Math at Hand

Teacher's Resource Book

GReaT SouRCe®

EDUCATION GROUP
A Houghton Mifflin Company
New Ways to Know®

Credits:

Design and Production: Taurins Design Associates

Illustration Credits:

Robot Characters: Inkwell Studios

Creative Art: Joe Spooner

Technical Art: Taurins Design Associates

Printed in the United States of America

Great Source® and *New Ways to Know®* are registered trademarks of Houghton Mifflin Company.

International Standard Book Number: 0-669-47230-1

3 4 5 6 7 8 9 10 MZ 04 03 02 01

Visit our website: http://www.greatsource.com/

Math at Hand is a reference handbook for students, teachers, and parents. It provides concise explanations and examples that are written on the student level. *Math at Hand*, with instructional support from teachers, is a tool that can empower students to become more responsible for their own learning, reviewing, relearning, research, and extended thinking.

TEACHER USES

Math at Hand is organized by topics, not by chapters. Some students may need only a quick review of dividing with fractions. Others may need to review all computational procedures with fractions. *Math at Hand* brings all those skills together in one section.

Vocabulary is an area of mathematics that is often overlooked or not emphasized. *Math at Hand* provides an avenue for a stronger approach to terms and their applications since it contains definitions and explanations that are easy to communicate to students. The use of vocabulary in instruction also provides ways for students who have difficulty with computation to excel through their understanding of verbal relationships and meanings.

STUDENT USES

Math at Hand provides a ready reference for students whose notes are unavailable, incomplete, or indecipherable when they are doing homework. There are times when textbook explanations need further clarification. *Math at Hand* gives clear explanations that allow students to understand a difficult topic more fully. The pictures, charts, and simple explanations fill gaps in learning that a student may have, but is unlikely to voice.

Student research is an important part of education. Students can easily access information in *Math at Hand* through various points of entry. They can look up a term in the glossary, found in the Yellow Pages section. The terms are cross-referenced to items in the main section of the handbook. Each section is color coded with a key on the back cover. The use of mathematically correct vocabulary along with the examples helps students connect words with symbols. The glossary provides a comprehensive resource of math terms.

PARENT USES

Math at Hand is a concise handbook of math topics that parents can readily use. Math textbooks usually have detailed explanations of single skills. *Math at Hand* presents those single skills in a larger context and connects concepts to previous learning. Many parents may find this a useful mechanism for recalling mathematical steps that have grown rusty over time.

The wide variety of diagrams and clear explanations in *Math at Hand* give parents a great resource to help with homework. Equipping parents to help improve their child's learning is a benefit that reaches far beyond the classroom.

The organization of this book parallels the sections of *Math at Hand*. You may first want to correlate the chapters of your textbook to the sections of *Math at Hand*. This will enable a ready reference to the practice and activities in this book. Each section may include more than one chapter of your text.

Math at Hand Teacher's Resource Book provides practice and test preparation pages for each sub-section of *Math at Hand*. These pages are followed by an answer page with answers to both the practice and test questions. Each section concludes with an application activity, designed to connect topics that relate to more than one area of mathematics.

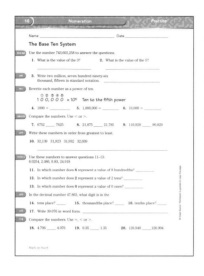

The practice pages are copymasters that follow the organization of each sub-section of *Math at Hand*. Each problem is cross-referenced to show students which item number(s) in *Math at Hand* will provide help, if needed. This feature also allows you to identify specific concepts that students may need help to understand. The practice pages can be assigned by sub-section in their entirety or by question number to accompany material recently covered.

The test preparation pages are copymasters that present the concepts of each sub-section of *Math at Hand* in a variety of standardized state test formats. This enables students to become familiar with question formats they may encounter when taking standardized tests. Students who have had experience with these formats often achieve higher test scores than students who have had no prior encounters with the types of questions used in standardized tests.

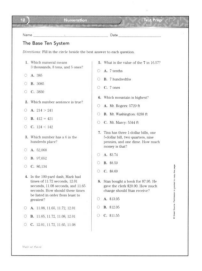

The application activities at the end of each section are designed to provide examples of mathematics as it relates to real-world situations. Some activities relate directly to daily tasks such as shopping and playing, while some involve using math manipulatives to reinforce concepts. Each application includes extension activities on the teacher page so that students may continue studies on the topic. Also in this book is a rubric that you may use for grading many of the activities.

At Your Fingertips

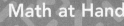

OBJECTIVE
- Explore the *Math at Hand* handbook to determine the format of the book

MATERIALS
- *Math at Hand* handbook
- Math Notebook Page, page 190

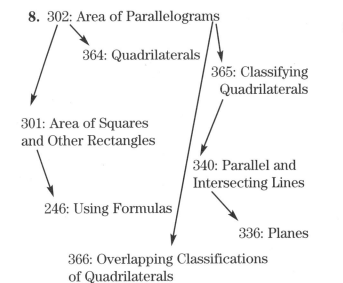

TIME
- 30 minutes

TEACHER NOTES
- This activity leads students on a tour through the *Math at Hand* handbook and enables them to become more familiar with the organization and features of the book. It also introduces them to the structure of the eleven application activities of this book.

- Have students correlate chapters of their textbook to the sections of *Math at Hand*. Often more than one chapter may relate to a section of the handbook.

EXTENSIONS
- Have students find four mathematical terms in the Glossary that are new to them. Have them write an explanation for each term in their own words, so they could explain the new terms to a friend.

- Have students select a topic and create a web of information.

ANSWERS
1. 14 including the Almanac, Yellow Pages, and Index

2. Each section has its own color.

3. Definitions, procedures, explanations, and rules are given as examples of things that might be looked up in *Math at Hand*.

4. Index: 299–308 and specific references for various plane figures

   Glossary: 299

   Table of Contents: 299

5. The Glossary

6. To show a quick way to multiply by multiples of 10 using mental math

7. ⭐ calls attention to the answer at the end of an explanation.

   ✳ calls attention to More Help messages, showing item numbers where additional help can be found.

   ❗ calls attention to Math Alert boxes, showing possible errors or misunderstandings.

8. 302: Area of Parallelograms

   364: Quadrilaterals

   365: Classifying Quadrilaterals

   301: Area of Squares and Other Rectangles

   340: Parallel and Intersecting Lines

   246: Using Formulas

   336: Planes

   366: Overlapping Classifications of Quadrilaterals

Name _____ Date _____

HANDBOOK HELP

This spot will list references to Math at Hand to help you find information you can use to solve the problems on the activity pages. This activity will help you discover how the Math at Hand handbook is organized.

At Your Fingertips

1. How many sections are there in *Math at Hand*? _____

2. How can you tell one section from another section?

_____

3. Find item number vii, "How This Book Is Organized." What four things might you want to look up in this book?

_____

4. Item number x, "How to Use This Book," shows three ways to find information about math topics. Look up *Area* in each of the three sections and write the item number(s) you find.

Index _____ Glossary _____ Table of Contents _____

5. Suppose you want to find definitions for the terms *factor* and *factorial*. What is the quickest place to look in *Math at Hand* to find the definitions?

_____

6. Take a look at the "Shortcut" box in item number 086. What is the purpose of the directions in the box?

_____

7. *Math at Hand* uses several symbols to call things to your attention. Write the meaning of each of these symbols.

⭐ _____

✴ _____

❗ _____

8. For many topics in *Math at Hand* there are More Help messages. These messages refer you to related topics, creating a web of information you can use. On your Math Notebook Page, start with item number 302, "Area of Parallelograms," and follow the path through the web for each item number until you have found all the new information. Draw arrows connecting each item number to the next.

Name _____ Date _____

	Gold	**Silver**	**Bronze**	**Copper**
Comprehension	Specific facts and relationships are identified and well-defined.	Most facts and relationships are defined.	Some facts are identified but relationships are missing.	No facts or relationships stated.
Application and Analysis	A strong plan is developed and executed correctly.	A plan is developed and implemented with some computational errors.	Some organized computation toward a weak plan.	Random computation with little relation to problem. No plan is present.
Mechanics	Appropriate and correct computation, mathematical representation, and graphics.	Appropriate computation that may be incorrect. Mathematical representation and graphics are present.	Computation is wrong and leads to further mistakes.	Computation is random. Mathematical representations are non-existent.
Presentation	Strong and succinct communication of results.	Strong communication of results. Justification for method may be weak.	Communication of results is present, but lacks any justification.	No results are communicated. No justification is to be found. A correct answer may have appeared.
Aesthetics	Exceptional. Attractive. Encourages attention. All requirements exceeded.	Neat and orderly. Requirements met.	Messy and disorganized. Some requirements missing.	Illegible and random information. Most requirements missing.

Name _____ Date _____

	Gold	Silver	Bronze	Copper
Do I know what to do?	I used the right numbers and the right plan.	I used some right numbers and an OK plan.	I used some right numbers but I need a plan.	I haven't got a clue.
Can I do it?	I got it all done and can defend my answer(s).	I got it all done and most of it is right.	I got some of it done and I think it's right.	I got some answers but I'm not sure they're right.
Is it right?	There are no mistakes. I think my pictures are great.	Oops! I made a couple of careless errors.	I made mistakes that messed up the other answers.	I can't tell if it's right.
Is my work clear?	Everyone could understand my work.	I may need to explain some of my work.	I'll definitely need to explain my work.	I hope no one asks me about my work.
How does it look?	Wow! Maybe I can help somebody else next time!	It could have been neater.	This looks really unorganized.	I should have asked for help.

Name _____ Date _____

The Base Ten System

004-005 Use the number 743,602,258 to answer the questions.

1. What is the value of the 3?   **2.** What is the value of the 5?

_____   _____

006 **3.** Write two million, seven hundred ninety-six thousand, fifteen in standard notation. _____

007 Rewrite each number as a power of ten.

① ② ③ ④ ⑤

$1\ 0\ 0,0\ 0\ 0 = 10^5$ *Ten to the fifth power*

4. 1000 = _____   **5.** 1,000,000 = _____   **6.** 10,000 = _____

008-009 Compare the numbers. Use < or >.

7. 6752 _____ 7625   **8.** 21,875 _____ 21,785   **9.** 110,928 _____ 90,829

010 Write these numbers in order from greatest to least.

10. 32,139   31,923   31,932   32,039

_____

011-012 Use these numbers to answer questions 11–13:
8.0254, 2.086, 0.83, 24.918

11. In which number does **8** represent a value of 8 hundredths? _____

12. In which number does **2** represent a value of 2 tens? _____

13. In which number does **0** represent a value of 0 ones? _____

013 In the decimal number 47.863, what digit is in the

14. tens place? _____   **15.** thousandths place? _____   **16.** tenths place? _____

014 **17.** Write 39.076 in word form. _____

016 Compare the numbers. Use =, < or >.

18. 4.706 _____ 4.076   **19.** 0.35 _____ 1.35   **20.** 126.940 _____ 126.904

Name _____ Date _____

018

Write these decimal numbers in order from least to greatest.

21. 20.987 2.098 209.87 0.209

_____

0.80   = $\frac{80}{100}$ = $\frac{8}{10}$ = $\frac{4}{5}$

Write each of these decimals as a fraction in simplest form.

019

22. 0.005 = _____   **23.** 0.40 = _____   **24.** 0.55 = _____

25. 0.17 = _____   **26.** 0.75 = _____   **27.** 0.04 = _____

38 of 100 squares
are shaded.
$\frac{38}{100}$ =

0.38 of the squares
are shaded.
0.38   =

38% of the squares
are shaded.
38%

Write each decimal as a percent.

020

28. 0.04 = _____   **29.** 1.00 = _____   **30.** 0.62 = _____

31. 0.80 = _____   **32.** 0.01 = _____   **33.** 0.23 = _____

Rewrite these decimals using a bar to show the digits that repeat.

021

34. 1.666...   _____   **35.** 12.454545... _____

36. 645.124124... _____   **37.** 53.3777...   _____

You have 2 five-dollar bills, 4 one-dollar bills, 2 quarters, 1 nickel, and 2 pennies.

024-025

38. What is the value of the bills? _____

39. What is the value of the coins? _____

40. How much money do you have? _____

Write the amount of change for each purchase.

026

41. Cost: $0.46   Cash: $1.00   **42.** Cost: $63.98   Cash: $100.00

    Change: _____   Change: _____

Name _____ Date _____

The Base Ten System

Directions: Fill in the circle beside the best answer to each question.

1. Which numeral means 3 thousands, 8 tens, and 5 ones?

   ○ **A.** 385

   ○ **B.** 3085

   ○ **C.** 3850

2. Which number sentence is true?

   ○ **A.** 214 > 241

   ○ **B.** 412 = 421

   ○ **C.** 124 < 142

3. Which number has a 6 in the hundreds place?

   ○ **A.** 52,068

   ○ **B.** 97,652

   ○ **C.** 86,134

4. In the 100-yard dash, Mark had times of 11.72 seconds, 12.01 seconds, 11.08 seconds, and 11.65 seconds. How should these times be listed in order from least to greatest?

   ○ **A.** 11.08, 11.65, 11.72, 12.01

   ○ **B.** 11.65, 11.72, 11.08, 12.01

   ○ **C.** 12.01, 11.72, 11.65, 11.08

5. What is the value of the **7** in 16.57?

   ○ **A.** 7 tenths

   ○ **B.** 7 hundredths

   ○ **C.** 7 ones

6. Which mountain is highest?

   ○ **A.** Mt. Rogers: 5729 ft

   ○ **B.** Mt. Washington: 6288 ft

   ○ **C.** Mt. Marcy: 5344 ft

7. Tina has three 1-dollar bills, one 5-dollar bill, two quarters, nine pennies, and one dime. How much money is that?

   ○ **A.** $3.74

   ○ **B.** $8.59

   ○ **C.** $8.69

8. Stan bought a book for $7.95. He gave the clerk $20.00. How much change should Stan receive?

   ○ **A.** $13.05

   ○ **B.** $12.05

   ○ **C.** $11.55

PRACTICE ANSWERS
Page 10

1. three million
2. fifty
3. 2,796,015
4. 10^3
5. 10^6
6. 10^4
7. 6752 < 7625
8. 21,875 > 21,785
9. 110,928 > 90,829
10. 32,139; 32,039; 31,932; 31,923
11. 2.086
12. 24.918
13. 0.83
14. 4
15. 3
16. 8
17. thirty-nine and seventy-six thousandths
18. 4.706 > 4.076
19. 0.35 < 1.35
20. 126.940 > 126.904

Page 11

21. 0.209; 2.098; 20.987; 209.87
22. $\frac{1}{200}$
23. $\frac{2}{5}$
24. $\frac{11}{20}$
25. $\frac{17}{100}$
26. $\frac{3}{4}$
27. $\frac{1}{25}$
28. 4%
29. 100%
30. 62%
31. 80%
32. 1%
33. 23%
34. $1.\overline{6}$
35. $12.\overline{45}$
36. $645.\overline{124}$
37. $53.3\overline{7}$
38. 14 dollars
39. 57 cents
40. $14.57
41. $0.54
42. $36.02

TEST PREP ANSWERS
Page 12

1. B
2. C
3. B
4. A
5. B
6. B
7. C
8. B

Name _____ Date _____

Fractions

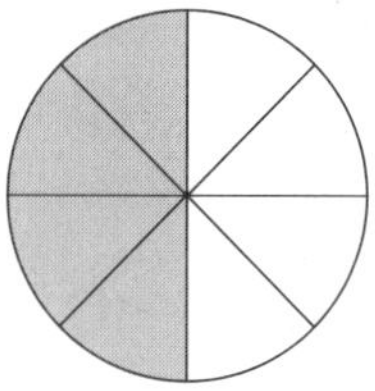

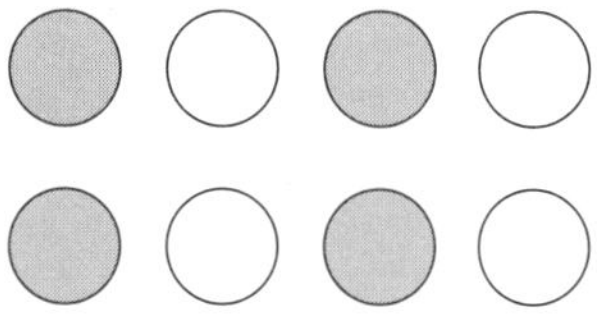

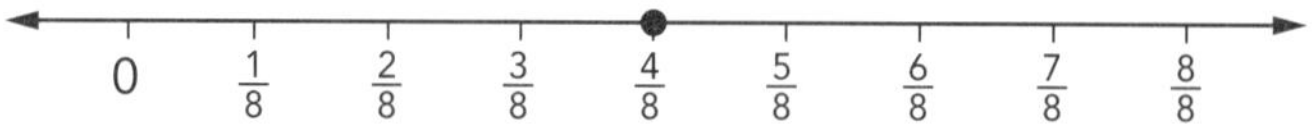

$$\frac{4}{8}\ \text{numerator}$$
$$\text{denominator}$$

028   **1.** Write a fraction for the shaded part. _____

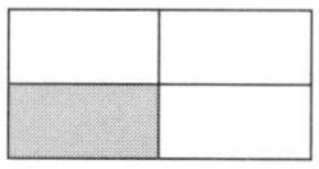

   2. What fraction of this figure is shaded? _____

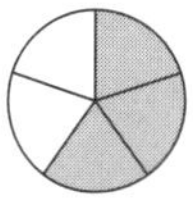

   3. Write a fraction for the shaded part. _____

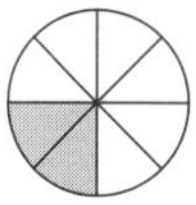

029   Write how you would say these fractions.

   4. $\frac{2}{3}$ _____

   5. $\frac{4}{15}$ _____

   6. $\frac{5}{9}$ _____

031   Name a fraction that is between

   7. $\frac{1}{4}$ and $\frac{1}{2}$. _____   **8.** $\frac{2}{3}$ and $\frac{3}{4}$. _____   **9.** $\frac{1}{3}$ and $\frac{1}{5}$. _____

033   **10.** Which picture shows $\frac{2}{3}$ of the boxes shaded? _____

     A. 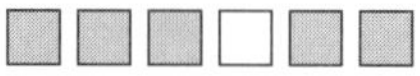   **B.**

     C. 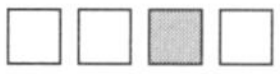   **D.**

034   **11.** What part of the fractions bars is shaded? _____

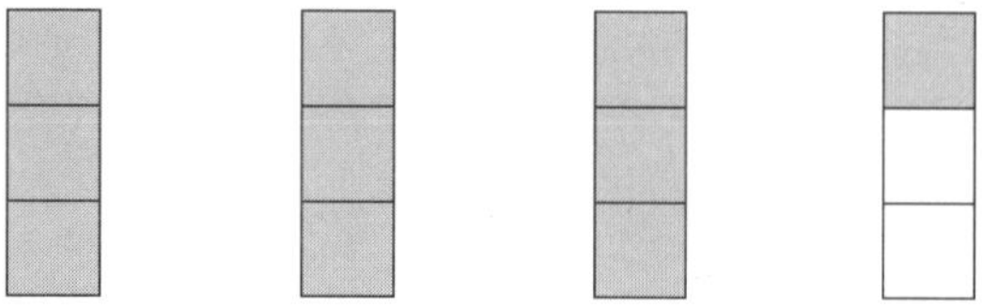

Name _____ Date _____

Write these fractions as mixed numbers.

12. $\frac{16}{5}$ = _____   **13.** $\frac{27}{11}$ = _____

$\frac{9}{4}$ = $4\overline{)9}$ with quotient 2, -8, remainder 1 $\frac{9}{4}$ = $2\frac{1}{4}$

14. $\frac{20}{8}$ = _____   **15.** $\frac{31}{5}$ = _____

16. Draw lines connecting equivalent fractions.

$\frac{1}{2}$ $\frac{2}{3}$

$\frac{4}{6}$ $\frac{4}{12}$

$\frac{3}{8}$ $\frac{6}{16}$

$\frac{1}{3}$ $\frac{3}{6}$

For each fraction write an equivalent fraction.

$\frac{9}{12} \div \boxed{1\frac{3}{3}} = \frac{3}{4}$ $\frac{1}{6} \times \boxed{1\frac{2}{2}} = \frac{2}{12}$

17. $\frac{2}{8}$ = _____   **18.** $\frac{1}{7}$ = _____   **19.** $\frac{2}{6}$ = _____

20. $\frac{15}{25}$ = _____   **21.** $\frac{3}{11}$ = _____   **22.** $\frac{1}{5}$ = _____

23. What is the least common denominator for the fractions $\frac{1}{4}$ and $\frac{3}{10}$? _____

Rewrite the fractions $\frac{1}{4}$ and $\frac{3}{10}$ using the least common denominator.

24. $\frac{1}{4}$ = _____   **25.** $\frac{3}{10}$ = _____

26. Compare the two fractions. Write a number sentence using $<$, $>$, or $=$.

_____

Write each fraction in simplest form.

27. $\frac{8}{12}$ _____   **28.** $\frac{4}{8}$ _____   **29.** $\frac{21}{28}$ _____   **30.** $\frac{24}{64}$ _____

31. $\frac{10}{30}$ _____   **32.** $\frac{12}{27}$ _____   **33.** $\frac{6}{24}$ _____   **34.** $\frac{16}{40}$ _____

Name _____ Date _____

039 Compare the fractions. Draw a line under the **smaller** fraction.

35. $\frac{1}{4}$ $\frac{2}{4}$ **36.** $\frac{5}{10}$ $\frac{8}{10}$ **37.** $\frac{13}{25}$ $\frac{11}{25}$

040 Write <, >, or =.

38. $\frac{1}{3}$ _____ $\frac{1}{2}$ **39.** $\frac{4}{5}$ _____ $\frac{12}{15}$ **40.** $\frac{2}{7}$ _____ $\frac{7}{14}$

41. $\frac{2}{3}$ _____ $\frac{4}{5}$ **42.** $\frac{5}{7}$ _____ $\frac{3}{9}$ **43.** $\frac{25}{100}$ _____ $\frac{5}{25}$

44. Which fraction is greater than $\frac{2}{3}$?

     A. $\frac{3}{4}$ **B.** $\frac{2}{5}$ **C.** $\frac{1}{2}$ **D.** $\frac{2}{6}$

45. Which fraction is less than $\frac{3}{8}$?

     A. $\frac{1}{4}$ **B.** $\frac{2}{3}$ **C.** $\frac{1}{2}$ **D.** $\frac{2}{5}$

Write *true* or *false* for each number sentence.

46. $\frac{1}{2} > \frac{3}{4}$ _____   **47.** $\frac{4}{6} = \frac{1}{3}$ _____   **48.** $\frac{3}{4} < \frac{7}{8}$ _____

49. $\frac{2}{3} > \frac{1}{2}$ _____   **50.** $\frac{3}{4} < \frac{4}{6}$ _____   **51.** $\frac{3}{15} = \frac{1}{5}$ _____

042 Write the mixed numbers in order from least to greatest.

52. $2\frac{3}{5}$ $2\frac{1}{10}$ $3\frac{1}{20}$ $2\frac{3}{4}$

043 Write a decimal for each fraction.

53. $\frac{4}{5}$ = _____   **54.** $\frac{45}{100}$ = _____   **55.** $\frac{10}{25}$ = _____

56. $\frac{3}{4}$ = _____   **57.** $\frac{7}{10}$ = _____   **58.** $\frac{17}{20}$ = _____

044 Write a fraction in simplest form for each percent.

59. 19% = _____   **60.** 90% = _____   **61.** 5% = _____

Write a percent for each fraction.

62. $\frac{13}{25}$ = _____   **63.** $\frac{8}{20}$ = _____   **64.** $\frac{3}{5}$ = _____

Name _____ Date _____

Fractions

Directions: Mark the letter beside the best answer to each question.

1 What part of this figure is shaded?

A $\frac{3}{4}$

B $\frac{2}{5}$

C $\frac{3}{5}$

D $\frac{1}{2}$

2 Mario made a pizza and cut it into 8 equal pieces. He and his friends ate 6 pieces. What fraction of the pizza did they eat?

F $\frac{2}{3}$

G $\frac{3}{4}$

H $\frac{1}{2}$

J $\frac{5}{8}$

3 Which fraction is greatest?

A $\frac{7}{8}$

B $\frac{1}{2}$

C $\frac{3}{4}$

D $\frac{2}{3}$

4 In the figure below, what part is shaded?

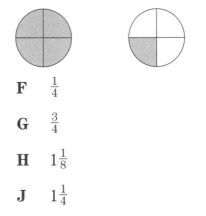

F $\frac{1}{4}$

G $\frac{3}{4}$

H $1\frac{1}{8}$

J $1\frac{1}{4}$

5 Marcy has 6 caps: 3 of the caps are red, 2 are green, and 1 is white. What fraction of the caps are red?

A $\frac{3}{5}$

B $\frac{1}{2}$

C $\frac{4}{6}$

D $\frac{1}{3}$

6 Which number sentence is true?

F $\frac{1}{3} > \frac{1}{4}$

G $\frac{2}{5} < \frac{1}{5}$

H $\frac{3}{4} > \frac{6}{8}$

J $\frac{4}{10} = \frac{1}{2}$

PRACTICE ANSWERS
Page 14

1. $\frac{1}{4}$

2. $\frac{3}{5}$

3. $\frac{2}{8}$ or $\frac{1}{4}$

4. two thirds

5. four fifteenths

6. five ninths

7. Answers will vary. $\frac{1}{3}$, $\frac{5}{12}$, and so on.

8. Answers will vary. $\frac{5}{7}$, $\frac{17}{24}$, and so on.

9. Answers will vary. $\frac{1}{4}$, $\frac{4}{15}$, and so on.

10. B

11. $3\frac{1}{3}$

Page 15

12. $3\frac{1}{5}$

13. $2\frac{5}{11}$

14. $2\frac{4}{8}$ or $2\frac{1}{2}$

15. $6\frac{1}{5}$

16.
$\frac{1}{2}$	$\frac{2}{3}$
$\frac{4}{6}$	$\frac{4}{12}$
$\frac{3}{8}$	$\frac{6}{16}$
$\frac{1}{3}$	$\frac{3}{6}$

17. Answers will vary. $\frac{1}{4}$, $\frac{4}{16}$, and so on.

18. Answers will vary. $\frac{2}{14}$, $\frac{4}{28}$, and so on.

19. Answers will vary. $\frac{1}{3}$, $\frac{4}{12}$, and so on.

20. Answers will vary. $\frac{3}{5}$, $\frac{6}{10}$, and so on.

21. Answers will vary. $\frac{6}{22}$, $\frac{9}{33}$, and so on.

22. Answers will vary. $\frac{2}{10}$, $\frac{3}{15}$, and so on.

23. 20

24. $\frac{5}{20}$

25. $\frac{6}{20}$

26. $\frac{5}{20} < \frac{6}{20}$ or $\frac{6}{20} > \frac{5}{20}$

27. $\frac{2}{3}$

28. $\frac{1}{2}$

29. $\frac{3}{4}$

30. $\frac{3}{8}$

31. $\frac{1}{3}$

32. $\frac{4}{9}$

33. $\frac{1}{4}$

34. $\frac{2}{5}$

Page 16

35. $\frac{1}{4}$

36. $\frac{5}{10}$

37. $\frac{11}{25}$

38. $\frac{1}{3} < \frac{1}{2}$

39. $\frac{4}{5} = \frac{12}{15}$

40. $\frac{2}{7} < \frac{7}{14}$

41. $\frac{2}{3} < \frac{4}{5}$

42. $\frac{5}{7} > \frac{3}{9}$

43. $\frac{25}{100} > \frac{5}{25}$

44. A

45. A

46. false

47. false

48. true

49. true

50. false

51. true

52. $2\frac{1}{10}, 2\frac{3}{5}, 2\frac{3}{4}, 3\frac{1}{20}$

53. 0.8

54. 0.45

55. 0.4

56. 0.75

57. 0.7

58. 0.85

59. $\frac{19}{100}$

60. $\frac{9}{10}$

61. $\frac{1}{20}$

62. 52%

63. 40%

64. 60%

TEST PREP ANSWERS
Page 17

1. C

2. G

3. A

4. J

5. B

6. F

Name _____ Date _____

Positive and Negative Numbers

Positive and negative numbers can be used to show amounts of money.

+$4   means you have money in your pocket.
⁻$4   means you owe a friend $4.

You can think about money to help you compare integers.

For example, which is greater, $2 or ⁻$3?
Think about money. You are better off if you have $2 than if you owe a friend $3.
So, $2 > ⁻3$.

Write an integer for each situation.

046

1. 5° colder than 0°: _____   **2.** 100 feet above sea level: _____

3. You have $5: _____   **4.** You owe a friend $8: _____

Compare each pair of integers. Write > or < in each blank. Use the number line to help you.

047

```
 ◄──┼────┼────┼────┼────┼────┼────┼────┼────●────┼────┼────┼────┼────┼────┼────┼────┼──►
   ⁻8   ⁻7   ⁻6   ⁻5   ⁻4   ⁻3   ⁻2   ⁻1    0    1    2    3    4    5    6    7    8
```

5. ⁻4 _____ 6   **6.** ⁻3 _____ ⁻2   **7.** 5 _____ ⁻1   **8.** 7 _____ ⁻3

9. 8 _____ 0   **10.** ⁻7 _____ 6   **11.** 0 _____ ⁻5   **12.** ⁻5 _____ ⁻8

Show the numbers on the number line. Then order them from least to greatest.

048

13. 5, ⁻5, 3, ⁻3

```
 ◄──┼────┼────┼────┼────┼────┼────┼────┼────●────┼────┼────┼────┼────┼────┼────┼────┼──►
```

14. From least to greatest: _____ _____ _____ _____

15. ⁻2, ⁻4, ⁻1, ⁻7

```
 ◄──┼────┼────┼────┼────┼────┼────┼────┼────●────┼────┼────┼────┼────┼────┼────┼────┼──►
```

16. From least to greatest: _____ _____ _____ _____

Name _____ Date _____

Positive and Negative Numbers

For a class project, Gina recorded the outside temperature each morning at 8:00 A.M. The temperatures are listed in the table below.

Outside Temperatures 8:00 A.M.	
Day	Temperature (F)
Feb. 1	2°
Feb. 2	⁻11°
Feb. 3	⁻5°
Feb. 4	3°
Feb. 5	⁻1°
Feb. 6	0°

1. Mark each temperature on the number line and label it with the date it was recorded.

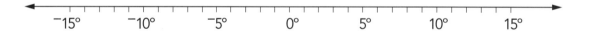

2. Which day had the lowest temperature at 8:00 A.M.?

_____

3. Write the temperatures in order from coldest to warmest.

_____

4. On which days was the recorded temperature above zero?

_____

PRACTICE ANSWERS
Page19

1. $^-5$
2. 100
3. 5
4. $^-8$
5. $^-4 < 6$
6. $^-3 < ^-2$
7. $5 > ^-1$
8. $7 > ^-3$
9. $8 > 0$
10. $^-7 < 6$
11. $0 > ^-5$
12. $^-5 > ^-8$
13.

14. $^-5, ^-3, 3, 5$
15.

16. $^-7, ^-4, ^-2, ^-1$

TEST PREP ANSWERS
Page 20

1.

2. Feb. 2
3. $^-11°, ^-5°, ^-1°, 0°, 2°, 3°$
4. Feb. 1 and Feb. 4

Piece It Together

OBJECTIVES
- Use tangrams to explore fractions
- Understand fraction of a whole and fraction of a set
- Relate fractions to percents

MATERIALS
- tangrams

TEACHER NOTES
- Students may need help constructing the square. They may use two same-size triangles to make a square and then stop. Make sure they know they need to use all seven tangram pieces.

- Talk about the relationship of fractions to percents. Remind students to think of percent as a fraction with a denominator of 100.

EXTENSIONS
- To emphasize the concept of ratio, assign a value of either one-half square unit or two square units to the small triangle. Have the students add columns to the chart and complete it for the new values. Then have them compare the fractions and discuss what they see.

- Students can make alphabet letters using tangram pieces. Assign values and have the students determine the area of the letters they make.

- Assign a value to one of the tangram pieces and have the students use it to measure the area of the front cover of the *Math at Hand* handbook.

ANSWERS
1. The tangram square is pictured below.

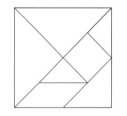

2.

Tangram Piece	Number of Small Triangle Pieces Needed to Cover
Small Triangle	1
Small Triangle	1
Medium Triangle	2
Square	2
Parallelogram	2
Large Triangle	4
Large Triangle	4
TOTAL	16

3. $\frac{1}{4}$ 10. $\frac{2}{7}$

4. $\frac{1}{8}$ 11. $\frac{1}{7}$

5. $\frac{1}{8}$ 12. $\frac{2}{7}$

6. $\frac{1}{16}$ 13. 5

7. $\frac{1}{2}$ 14. $\frac{5}{7}$

8. 50%   15. $\frac{3}{4}$

9. 2   16. 75%

Name _____ Date _____

HANDBOOK
HELP

Fraction of a Whole: 030

Fraction of a Set: 033

Simplest Form: 037

Relating Fractions to
Percents: 044

Piece It Together

1. Make a square using all seven tangram pieces.
Then sketch it on the back of this page.

2. Use one of the small triangles as a unit of measure to
cover each of the other pieces. Record your answers in
the chart below. Then add up all the pieces to find the
total needed to cover your square.

When you answer these questions, write
all fractions in simplest form.

Tangram Piece	Number of Small Triangle Pieces Needed to Cover
Small Triangle	1
Small Triangle	
Medium Triangle	
Square	
Parallelogram	
Large Triangle	
Large Triangle	
TOTAL	

3. What fraction of your tangram
square is one large triangle? _____

4. What fraction of your tangram
square is the parallelogram? _____

5. What fraction of your tangram
square is the medium triangle? _____

6. What fraction of your tangram
square is one small triangle? _____

7. What fraction of your tangram square
are the two large triangles together? _____

8. What percent of your tangram square
are the two large triangles together? _____

9. You made the square using seven tangram pieces.
How many of those pieces are small triangles? _____

10. What fraction of the tangram pieces is that? _____

11. What fraction of the pieces is the small square? _____

12. What fraction of the pieces are large triangles? _____

13. How many of the pieces in your square are triangles? _____

14. What fraction of the pieces are triangles? _____

15. You have four coins totaling 25 cents.
What fraction of the coins are nickels? _____

16. What percent of the coins are nickels? _____

Name _____ Date _____

Factors and Multiples

051 Write three pairs of factors of 48.

1. _____ 2. _____ 3. _____

4. Write all the factors of 52. _____

$$5! = 5 \times 4 \times 3 \times 2 \times 1 = 120$$

052 Solve these problems in the same way.

5. $6! =$ _____ = _____

6. $9! =$ _____ = _____

053, 055 For each number, write all its factors and identify it as prime or composite.

7. 51 _____ prime   composite

8. 101 _____ prime   composite

9. 85 _____ prime   composite

10. 119 _____ prime   composite

056 Write the prime factors of each number. Use factor trees.

11.   75   12.   38

13.   80   14.   189

Name _____ Date _____

Write the prime factorization of each number. Use exponents when possible.

056

15. 36 _____

16. 42 _____

17. 50 _____

18. Which of these shows the prime factorization of **175**? _____

　　A. 5×35　　　　　　**B.** $5 \times 5 \times 7$　　　　　　**C.** $1 \times 5 \times 5 \times 7$

Write the factors of the numbers. Then circle the common factors.

057

19. 70 _____

20. 84 _____

21. What are the common factors of 12, 54, and 60? _____

22. What is the greatest common factor of 12, 54, and 60? _____

058

Write the factors of the numbers. Then circle the common factors.

23. 21 _____

24. 51 _____

25. What is the greatest common factor of 21 and 51? _____

26. What is the greatest common factor of 45 and 48? _____

27. What is the greatest common factor of 16, 28, and 40? _____

28. List the first eight multiples of 3. _____

059

29. List the first five multiples of 7. _____

30. What is the least common multiple of 3 and 7? _____

061

31. What is the least common multiple of 6 and 15? _____

32. What is the least common multiple of 2, 4, and 5? _____

33. What is the least common multiple of 3, 4, and 5? _____

Name _____ Date _____

062 Use the divisibility table in *Math at Hand* item 062 to help you answer these questions.

34. Is 285 divisible by 5? _____ How do you know? _____

_____

35. Is 1035 divisible by 4? _____ How do you know? _____

_____

36. Is 11,706 divisible by 6? _____ How do you know? _____

_____

Solve the next two problems mentally.

37. There are 156 marbles to share among 9 friends. Can you equally share them? ____

38. Marbles are sold in packages of 30 at the local store. How many packages

would you need to buy so all 9 people could equally share them? _____

063 **39.** Draw a circle around all the odd numbers. Draw a box around all the even numbers.

$$4,675,890 \qquad 2465 \qquad 34 \qquad 557$$

$$220,654 \qquad 71,329 \qquad 8883$$

Choose any two of these numbers that when added will result in an even number.

40. _____, _____

Choose any two of these numbers that when added will result in an odd number.

41. _____, _____

Name _____ Date _____

Factors and Multiples

Directions: Mark the letter beside the best answer to each question.

1. Which is a prime number?

   A. 9

   B. 16

   C. 25

   D. 31

2. Which is a composite number?

   A. 17

   B. 18

   C. 19

   D. 23

3. What is the greatest common factor of 16 and 24?

   A. 4

   B. 6

   C. 8

   D. 12

4. Which is an odd number?

   A. 107

   B. 120

   C. 114

   D. 152

Directions: Write the answer to each question.

5. Find all the factors of 28.

6. Find the LCM of 5 and 7.

7. Frank has chosen a number that is between 35 and 60. Both digits in the number are odd. When the two digits are added together, the sum is 6. The number has exactly four factors. What is the number?

8. There are 139 people waiting for a train. Each row of seats on the train can seat 4 people. Will all the rows be full? Explain.

PRACTICE ANSWERS
Page 24

1–3. Possible answers include 1×48, 2×24, 3×16, 4×12, or 6×8.

4. 1, 2, 4, 13, 26, 52

5. $6 \times 5 \times 4 \times 3 \times 2 \times 1 = 720$

6. $9 \times 8 \times 7 \times 6 \times 5 \times 4 \times 3 \times 2 \times 1 = 362{,}880$

7. 1, 3, 17, 51; composite

8. 1, 101; prime

9. 1, 5, 17, 85; composite

10. 1, 7, 17, 119; composite

11.
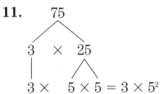

12.
$$\begin{array}{c} 38 \\ \diagup\ \diagdown \\ 2\quad \times\quad 19 \end{array}$$

13.
$$80$$
$$8 \times 10$$
$$2 \times 4 \times 2 \times 5$$
$$2 \times 2 \times 2 \times 2 \times 5 = 2^4 \times 5$$

14.
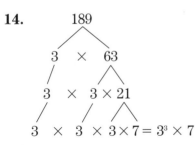

Page 25

15. $2^2 \times 3^2$

16. $2 \times 3 \times 7$

17. 2×5^2

18. B

19. ①,②, 5,⑦, 10,⑭, 35, 70

20. ①,②, 3, 4, 6,⑦, 12,⑭, 21, 28, 42, 84

21. 1, 2, 3, and 6

22. 6

23. ①,③, 7, 21

24. ①,③, 17, 51

25. 3

26. 3

27. 4

28. 3, 6, 9, 12, 15, 18, 21, 24

29. 7, 14, 21, 28, 35

30. 21

31. 30

32. 20

33. 60

Page 26

34. Yes. The ones digit is 5.

35. No. The number formed by the last two digits is not divisible by 4.

36. Yes. It is an even number (divisible by 2) and the sum of the digits is 15 (divisible by 3), so it is divisible by 6.

37. No

38. 2

39. | 4,675,890 | (2465) | 34 | (557) |
220,654 | (71,329) | (8883) |

40. Answers include any two even numbers or any two odd numbers from the list.

41. Answers include any combination of one odd and one even number from the list.

TEST PREP ANSWERS
Page 27

1. D

2. B

3. C

4. A

5. 1, 2, 4, 7, 14, 28

6. 35

7. 51

8. No, because 139 is not divisible by 4. One row will have only 3 people.

Name _____ Date _____

Powers and Roots

1. Use exponential form to show 5 used as a factor 4 times. _____ 065

2. Write eight to the fourth power in exponential form. _____

3. In 7^3, which digit is the base of the exponent? _____

4. What is the value of 8^3? _____

5. Write how you would say 10^6. _____

6. What is the value of $2^3 \times 3^2$? _____

7. $3^4 - 4^3 = $ _____   8. $2^2 \times 5^2 = $ _____   9. $3^3 + 7^2 = $ _____   065-066

10. $10^2 \times 2^2 = $ _____   11. $5^3 + 9^2 = $ _____   12. $7^2 - 6^0 = $ _____

Write *true* or *false* for each number sentence.   067

13. $\sqrt{25} + \sqrt{36} = 12$ _____   14. $\sqrt{16} \times \sqrt{144} = 48$ _____

15. $\sqrt{64} = 8^2$ _____   16. $\sqrt{49} + \sqrt{16} = 11$ _____

17. $2^2 + \sqrt{81} = 13$ _____   18. $\sqrt{9} - \sqrt{4} = 2$ _____

Use the Squares and Roots table in item 484 to answer these questions.   069

19. What is the square root of 79? _____

20. What is the square of 45? _____

21. What is the square root of 2? _____

22. What is the square root of 50? _____

23. What is the square of 27? _____

24. Circle all the perfect powers.   070

39   225   35   400   49

200   121   101   15

9   144   89

1000   12

81

Name _____   Date _____

Powers and Roots

Directions: Mark the letter beside the best answer to each question.

1. $6^3 =$

   A. 3×6

   B. 6×3

   C. $3 \times 3 \times 3 \times 3 \times 3 \times 3$

   D. $6 \times 6 \times 6$

2. Which notation is equal to 16?

   A. 4^4

   B. 2^4

   C. 8^2

   D. 2^8

3. How is the product $3 \times 3 \times 5 \times 5 \times 5$ expressed in exponential notation?

   A. $3^3 \times 5^4$

   B. $2^3 \times 3^5$

   C. $3^2 \times 5^3$

   D. 15^5

4. $12^0 =$

   A. 1

   B. 12

   C. 24

   D. 144

5. What is the square root of 25?

   A. 625

   B. 25

   C. 5

   D. 1

6. Which of these numbers is a perfect square?

   A. 35

   B. 40

   C. 44

   D. 49

7. 4^3 is equal to what number?

   A. 12

   B. 16

   C. 64

   D. 256

8. $\sqrt{100} =$

   A. 10

   B. 20

   C. 50

   D. 1000

PRACTICE ANSWERS
Page 29

1. 5^4
2. 8^4
3. 7
4. 512
5. ten to the sixth power
6. 72
7. 17
8. 100
9. 76
10. 400
11. 206
12. 48
13. false
14. true
15. false
16. true
17. true
18. false
19. 8.888
20. 2025
21. 1.414
22. 7.071
23. 729
24. Of the numbers listed, 225, 400, 49, 121, 9, 144, and 81 are perfect powers.

TEST PREP ANSWERS
Page 30

1. D
2. B
3. C
4. A
5. C
6. D
7. C
8. A

Divide and Conquer

OBJECTIVE
• Use rules for divisibility to determine dates in history

MATERIALS
• calculators (optional)

TIME
• 45–60 minutes

TEACHER NOTES
• These number puzzles give students the opportunity to reinforce what they may be learning about important dates in history.

• Encourage the students to analyze each clue carefully to eliminate as many numbers as possible. They can check each solution with a calculator for all divisibility rules given.

EXTENSIONS
• You may want to give the students a famous date in history and have them write a divisibility puzzle for the year. One example might be the assassination of Abraham Lincoln in 1865.

• Have the students write a divisibility puzzle for the year they were born. You may want to include the month and date as well.

• Research one of the events used and have the students write a paragraph about the importance of the event.

ANSWERS
1. 15_ _ is the starting place. The next clue leaves only the years 1500, 1521, 1542, 1563, and 1584 as solutions. Since the number is divisible by 2, all odd numbers can be eliminated. The remaining numbers can be checked for divisibility by 9 to arrive at the year 1584.

2. The first clue determines that the year is an even number. The second clue gives the digit in the hundreds place as 8. The third clue gives the digit in the tens place as 7. The difference between these two numbers gives the 1 in the thousands place. The last clue leaves only the years 1870, 1874, 1876, and 1878. Applying the divisibility rule for 4 from the first clue leaves only the correct answer, 1876.

3. The first clue gives 19_ _ as the starting place. The second clue determines that the digit in the ones place is 9. The next clue leaves only 1969 and 1999 as possibilities. The last clue leaves only the correct answer, 1969.

Name _____ Date _____

Whole Numbers:
   Place Value: 004
Prime Numbers: 053
Divisibility: 062
Division: 144–153

Divide and Conquer

A few historical events are listed below. Your job is to use number clues to figure out in what year they happened. Here's an example.

In what year was the Declaration of Independence written? It was written in the 1700s. (The year is 17_ _.) The digit in the tens place is a prime number between 3 and 8. (The digit in the tens place is either 5 or 7.) The year is divisible by 2, 3, 4, 6, and 8, but the digit in the ones place is not a 2. (The year must be an even number ending in 0, 4, 6, or 8.) The last two digits are divisible only by 2 and 4. (Of the remaining possibilities for the last two digits, only 56 and 76 are divisible by 4.) Apply the divisibility rules. Only 1776 works!

Try these.

1. In what year did Queen Elizabeth I give Sir Walter Raleigh permission to establish colonies in North America? It happened in the 1500s. The digit in the tens place is double the digit in the ones place. The year is divisible by 2, 3, 4, 6, 8, and 9.

   What year was it? _____

2. In what year did Alexander Graham Bell invent the telephone? The year is divisible only by 2 and by 4. The digit in the hundreds place is the product of 2 and 4. The digit in the tens place is a prime number between 5 and 9. The digit in the thousands place is the difference between the digits in the hundreds and tens places. The digit in the ones place is not 2.

   What year was it? _____

3. In what year did Neil Armstrong become the first person to walk on the moon? It happened in the 1900s. The year is one less than a number divisible by 2 and by 5. The last three digits are each divisible by 3, but 3 does not appear in the number. The last three digits are not all the same number.

   What year was it? _____

Name _____ Date _____

Mental Math

To add using mental math, look for combinations that need no regrouping, or that regroup to make ten.

To subtract using mental math, adjust the numbers so that they need no regrouping, or so that only 1-digit numbers are subtracted from the tens.

ONE WAY $95 - 47$

$95 - 45 - 2$

$50 - 2 = 48$

You need to subtract 2 more than 45.

ANOTHER WAY $95 - 47$

$95 - 50 + 3$

$45 + 3 = 48$

Subtracting 50 is subtracting 3 too many

073-076 Add. Use mental math.

1. $10 + 26 =$ _____   **2.** $49 + 41 =$ _____   **3.** $98 + 42 =$ _____

4. $27 + 34 =$ _____   **5.** $82 + 44 =$ _____   **6.** $37 + 39 =$ _____

7. $105 + 113 =$ _____   **8.** $126 + 85 =$ _____   **9.** $213 + 77 =$ _____

10. $197 + 156 =$ _____ **11.** $225 + 178 =$ _____ **12.** $144 + 266 =$ _____

077 Add using mental math. Decide which two numbers you will add first.

13. $5 + 9 + 7 + 3 + 7 =$ _____   **14.** $14 + 23 + 6 + 17 =$ _____

15. $21 + 27 + 14 =$ _____   **16.** $33 + 19 + 27 =$ _____

078-082 Subtract. Use mental math.

17. $48 - 19 =$ _____   **18.** $57 - 29 =$ _____   **19.** $42 - 18 =$ _____

20. $72 - 25 =$ _____   **21.** $56 - 38 =$ _____   **22.** $95 - 63 =$ _____

23. $83 - 36 =$ _____   **24.** $136 - 29 =$ _____   **25.** $125 - 97 =$ _____

Name _____ Date _____

69 × 5

$69 \times 5 = (69 \times 10) \div 2$
$= 690 \div 2$
$= 345$

72 ÷ 2

Since 72 has an odd number of tens, think of it as 6 tens and 12 ones. Then:
$72 \div 2 = (60 + 12) \div 2$
$= 30 + 6 = 36$

Multiply or divide by 2, 5, or 10. Use mental math.

090-091

26. $46 \div 2 =$ _____   **27.** $98 \div 2 =$ _____   **28.** $74 \div 2 =$ _____

29. $19 \times 10 =$ _____   **30.** $260 \div 10 =$ _____   **31.** $32 \times 5 =$ _____

32. $56 \times 5 =$ _____   **33.** $260 \div 5 =$ _____   **34.** $545 \div 5 =$ _____

23 × 8

$23 \times 8 = 23 \times 2 \times 2 \times 2$
$= 46 \times 2 \times 2$
$= 92 \times 2 = 184$

15 × 48

$15 \times 48 = (10 + 5) \times 48$
$= 480 + 240 = 720$

Multiply. Use mental math.

083-088

35. $24 \times 9 =$ _____   **36.** $15 \times 8 =$ _____   **37.** $33 \times 8 =$ _____

38. $42 \times 9 =$ _____   **39.** $22 \times 12 =$ _____   **40.** $35 \times 14 =$ _____

41. $35 \times 100 =$ _____   **42.** $35 \times 1000 =$ _____   **43.** $70 \times 200 =$ _____

44. $60 \times 500 =$ _____   **45.** $900 \times 900 =$ _____   **46.** $30 \times 8000 =$ _____

Divide. Use mental math.

089-092

47. $24,000 \div 60 =$ _____   **48.** $1600 \div 100 =$ _____

49. $25,000 \div 100 =$ _____   **50.** $4800 \div 60 =$ _____

51. $54,000 \div 900 =$ _____   **52.** $630 \div 70 =$ _____

53. $434 \div 100 =$ _____   **54.** $65 \div 1000 =$ _____

55. $1.2 \div 100 =$ _____   **56.** $233 \div 1000 =$ _____

Name _____ Date _____

Mental Math

Directions: Use mental math to solve each problem. Write your answers.

(**1**) Jane and Carla played nine holes of mini-golf. They wrote their scores on the card. What was the total score for each player?

Hole	1	2	3	4	5	6	7	8	9	Total
Jane	3	2	5	3	2	4	5	4	2	
Carla	2	3	3	4	2	5	5	3	1	

(**2**) Clarence got 120 raffle tickets to sell. He sold 97. How many tickets did he have left? _____

(**3**) Mr. Kato had to drive 297 miles to Buffalo. By noon, he had driven 88 miles. How many miles did he have left? _____

(**4**) There were 10 people in a club. Each member of the club made 64 cookies for a bake sale. How many cookies did they make in all? _____

(**5**) Helga rode her bike 22 miles per day for 9 days. How many miles did she ride in all? _____

(**6**) A total of 32,000 people gathered in the park and formed up into 8 equal groups. How many people were in each group? _____

PRACTICE ANSWERS
Page 34
1. 36
2. 90
3. 140
4. 61
5. 126
6. 76
7. 218
8. 211
9. 290
10. 353
11. 403
12. 410
13. 31
14. 60
15. 62
16. 79
17. 29
18. 28
19. 24
20. 47
21. 18
22. 32
23. 47
24. 107
25. 28

Page 35
26. 23
27. 49
28. 37
29. 190
30. 26
31. 160
32. 280
33. 52
34. 109
35. 216
36. 120
37. 264
38. 378
39. 264
40. 490
41. 3500
42. 35,000
43. 14,000
44. 30,000
45. 810,000
46. 240,000
47. 400
48. 16
49. 250
50. 80
51. 60
52. 9
53. 4.34
54. 0.065
55. 0.012
56. 0.233

TEST PREP ANSWERS
Page 36
1. Jane 30, Carla 28
2. 23
3. 209
4. 640
5. 198
6. 4000

Name _____ Date _____

Estimation

103-104, 109

Make a front-end estimate of each sum, difference, or product.
Then make an adjusted estimate.

	Front-end estimate	**Adjusted estimate**
$1256 + 766$	$1200 + 700 = 1900$	$1900 + 50 + 60 = 2010$
442×303	$400 \times 300 = 120{,}000$	$120{,}000 + (40 \times 300) = 132{,}000$

1. $556 + 192$ _____ _____

2. $131 + 844$ _____ _____

3. $736 - 258$ _____ _____

4. $1255 - 935$ _____ _____

5. 536×18 _____ _____

6. 478×516 _____ _____

101, 105, 107, 111

Estimate each sum, difference or product. Use rounding or compatible numbers. Show the rounded or compatible numbers you are using.

$$1752 \longrightarrow 1800$$
$$-944 \longrightarrow -900$$
$$900$$

$$7316 \longrightarrow 7000$$
$$\times 495 \longrightarrow \times 500$$
$$3{,}500{,}000$$

7. $695 \longrightarrow$ 8. $1236 \longrightarrow$ 9. $3440 \longrightarrow$
$+413 \longrightarrow +$____ $+452 \longrightarrow +$____ $-1756 \longrightarrow -$____

10. $95{,}512 \longrightarrow$ 11. $457 \longrightarrow$ 12. $68 \longrightarrow$
$- 63{,}101 \longrightarrow -$____ $\times 32 \longrightarrow \times$____ $\times 43 \longrightarrow \times$____

113-114

Estimate each quotient. Show the divisor and the dividend you are using.

13. $495 \div 12 \longrightarrow$ _____ $\div$ _____ $=$ _____

14. $572 \div 33 \longrightarrow$ _____ $\div$ _____ $=$ _____

15. $1258 \div 89 \longrightarrow$ _____ $\div$ _____ $=$ _____

16. $49{,}024 \div 651 \longrightarrow$ _____ $\div$ _____ $=$ _____

Name _____ Date _____

To estimate the sum or difference of two mixed numbers, first decide
whether each fraction is closer to a benchmark of 0, $\frac{1}{2}$, or 1.

$$8\frac{3}{8} + 4\frac{4}{5} \longrightarrow 8\frac{1}{2} + 5 = 13\frac{1}{2} \qquad\qquad 6\frac{5}{6} - 1\frac{2}{5} \longrightarrow 7 - 1\frac{1}{2} = 5\frac{1}{2}$$

Estimate each sum or difference. Show the benchmarks you are using.   098, 102

17. $1\frac{2}{5} + \frac{7}{8} \longrightarrow$ _____ + _____ = _____

18. $1\frac{7}{8} + 2\frac{1}{5} \longrightarrow$ _____ + _____ = _____

19. $6\frac{3}{5} - 2\frac{3}{4} \longrightarrow$ _____ − _____ = _____

20. $6\frac{7}{8} - 4\frac{1}{16} \longrightarrow$ _____ − _____ = _____

21. $9\frac{7}{10} + 6\frac{2}{5} \longrightarrow$ _____ + _____ = _____

22. $12\frac{7}{16} - 9\frac{5}{12} \longrightarrow$ _____ − _____ = _____

Estimate each product. Show the benchmarks you are using.   098, 108

23. $\frac{5}{8} \times 8\frac{1}{3} \longrightarrow$ _____ × _____ = _____

24. $1\frac{1}{4} \times 5\frac{3}{10} \longrightarrow$ _____ × _____ = _____

25. $2\frac{1}{5} \times 7\frac{2}{3} \longrightarrow$ _____ × _____ = _____

26. $3\frac{5}{6} \times 9\frac{1}{6} \longrightarrow$ _____ × _____ = _____

27. $8\frac{5}{12} \times 3\frac{1}{3} \longrightarrow$ _____ × _____ = _____

28. $9\frac{11}{12} \times 11\frac{7}{16} \longrightarrow$ _____ × _____ = _____

Estimate each percent of the number. Use benchmarks   099, 116
of 10%, 25%, 50%, 75%, and 100%.

43% of 250 ⟶ 50% of 250 = 125

29. 27% of 69 ⟶ _____ of _____ = _____

30. 97% of 26.5 ⟶ _____ of _____ = _____

31. 12% of 39 ⟶ _____ of _____ = _____

32. 56.5% of 93 ⟶ _____ of _____ = _____

33. 73% of 125 ⟶ _____ of _____ = _____

34. 8% of 1205 ⟶ _____ of _____ = _____

Name _____ Date _____

Estimation

Directions: Mark the letter beside the best answer to each question.

1. The height of the Amoco Building in Chicago is 1136 feet. What is the height rounded to the nearest hundred?

   A. 1000 ft

   B. 1100 ft

   C. 1200 ft

   D. 1300 ft

2. A farmer has 293 ducks and 105 geese. Which is the best estimate of the total number of birds?

   A. 4000

   B. 3000

   C. 400

   D. 300

3. A theater has 22 rows of seats. Each row has 28 seats. Which numbers would give the best estimate of the total number of seats?

   A. 20 × 20

   B. 30 × 30

   C. 25 × 30

   D. 20 × 30

4. A Max computer costs $1299.50. A Peach computer costs $919.95. About how much less does the Peach computer cost?

   A. $400

   B. $500

   C. $1000

   D. $2200

5. Edwin bought $18\frac{7}{10}$ gallons of gasoline at 1.19\frac{9}{10}$ per gallon. About how much did the gasoline cost?

   A. $10

   B. $15

   C. $20

   D. $24

6. On Friday, the ticket seller at the football stadium collected $6395 for 788 tickets. About how much did each ticket cost?

   A. $8

   B. $9

   C. $80

   D. $90

PRACTICE ANSWERS
Page 38

1. $500 + 100 = 600$;
   $600 + 50 + 90 = 740$
2. $100 + 800 = 900$;
   $900 + 30 + 40 = 970$
3. $700 - 200 = 500$;
   $730 - 250 = 480$
4. $1200 - 900 = 300$;
   $1250 - 930 = 320$
5. $500 \times 10 = 5000$;
   $500 \times 18 = 9000$
6. $400 \times 500 = 200{,}000$;
   $480 \times 500 = 240{,}000$
7. $700 + 400 = 1100$
8. $1200 + 400 = 1600$
9. $3400 - 1700 = 1700$
10. $100{,}000 - 60{,}000 = 40{,}000$
11. $500 \times 30 = 15{,}000$
12. $70 \times 40 = 2800$
13. $480 \div 12 = 40$
14. $600 \div 30 = 20$
15. $1300 \div 100 = 13$
16. $49{,}000 \div 700 = 70$

Page 39

17. $1\frac{1}{2} + 1 = 2\frac{1}{2}$
18. $2 + 2 = 4$
19. $6\frac{1}{2} - 3 = 3\frac{1}{2}$
20. $7 - 4 = 3$
21. $9\frac{1}{2} + 6\frac{1}{2} = 16$
22. $12\frac{1}{2} - 9\frac{1}{2} = 3$
23. $\frac{1}{2} \times 8 = 4$
24. $1 \times 5\frac{1}{2} = 5\frac{1}{2}$
25. $2 \times 8 = 16$
26. $4 \times 9 = 36$
27. $8\frac{1}{2} \times 3 = 25\frac{1}{2}$
28. $10 \times 11\frac{1}{2} = 115$
29. 25% of $68 = 17$
30. 100% of $27 = 27$
31. 10% of $40 = 4$
32. 50% of $90 = 45$
33. 75% of $120 = 90$
34. 10% of $1200 = 120$

TEST PREP ANSWERS
Page 40

1. B
2. C
3. D
4. A
5. D
6. A

When Is Enough Enough?

TIME
• 30–45 minutes

OBJECTIVE
• Estimate quantities of items to be ordered for the school store

MATERIALS
none

TEACHER NOTES

• The Glossary of Mathematical Terms in *Math at Hand* gives two definitions for the word *estimate*. Discuss the meanings, pointing out the different pronunciations for the noun and verb forms of the word.

• Point out to the students that choosing good numbers to arrive at an estimate is just as important as being close to the actual amount.

EXTENSIONS

• Use this table of costs for each item mentioned in the activity. By asking the students how much the purchase of each item will cost the store manager, the estimation activity can be extended. Continue to have the students write the numbers they use to make their estimates, as well as a brief explanation.

Assignment books	$3.12 each
Pencils	$24.50 per gross
Drawing pencils	$2.45 per set
Dictionaries	$5.71 each
Computer disks	$4.49 per box of 10
Bumper stickers	$125.00 per package of 100

• Students can use calculators to determine the actual amounts involved in each situation.

• Give the students an annual budget amount for the school store and ask them to determine if the manager will have enough money to buy the desired quantities of all the items.

• Select a profit margin and have the students determine the selling price and the estimated profit for the school store if all items are sold.

ANSWERS

Since the activity involves estimation, answers will vary. Check that students are choosing good numbers to use when making their estimates.

1. Good estimate: 800 assignment books; good numbers: 400 + 400, or 425 + 375

2. Good estimate: 290 bumper stickers; good numbers: 90% of 100 (90) + 25% of 800 (200)

3. Good estimate: 200 boxes; good numbers: 25% of 800

4. Good estimate: 400 sets; good numbers: 75% of 400 (300) + 25% of 400 (100)

5. Good estimate: 250 dictionaries; good numbers: about $\frac{1}{3}$ of 800

6. Good estimate: 12 gross; good numbers: 1600 pencils needed. 10 gross (1440) is not enough; 2 more gross are needed to have more than 1600 pencils.

Name _____ Date _____

When Is Enough Enough?

The Kimball School Store sells school supplies to the students and teachers. There are 429 fifth graders, 377 sixth graders, and 96 teachers. The manager is using information from previous years to figure out how many of each item to order.

Make an estimate for each situation. Write the numbers you use to make your estimate.

Handbook Help

Estimation: 093

Rounding Whole
Numbers: 095

Benchmark Percents:
099

Rounding to Estimate
Sums and Differences:
101

Front-End Estimation
of Products: 109

1. Each student is required to buy an assignment book each year. About how many should the manager order?

   Estimate: _____ The numbers I used: _____

2. About 90% of the teachers and 25% of the students buy school spirit bumper stickers each year. About how many bumper stickers should be ordered?

   Estimate: _____ The numbers I used: _____

3. Last year, about 23% of the students bought a box of ten computer disks at the store. About how many boxes should be ordered for this year?

   Estimate: _____ The numbers I used: _____

4. 75% of the fifth graders and 25% of the sixth graders take art each year and need to buy a set of drawing pencils. About how many sets should be ordered?

   Estimate: _____ The numbers I used: _____

5. Less than one-third of all students usually buy a dictionary. About how many should be ordered?

   Estimate: _____ The numbers I used: _____

6. Almost every student will buy at least two pencils during the year. The manager must buy the pencils by the gross. How many gross must she order?

   Estimate: _____ The numbers I used: _____

Name _____ Date _____

Addition

120 Rewrite and solve each problem. Be sure to line up the digits by place value.

1. 237 + 52   **2.** 604 + 321   **3.** 2186 + 310   **4.** 3007 + 5212

+ _____   + _____   + _____   + _____

121-122 Solve each problem.

5.	207	**6.**	4024	**7.**
	+136		+387	

5.   207
      +136

6.   4024
      +387

7.   860
      +253

8.   12,475
      +1,144

9.   7236
      +2769

10. 47,021
      +3,990

11. 6814
      +107

12. 75,805
      +16,497

123 Use subtraction to check these addition problems.
Write the correct answer for each problem.

13.   391   515
      + 124   − _____
       515

correct answer: _____

14.   1240
      +3582   − _____
       5822

correct answer: _____

15. 10,834
      + 2,420   − _____
      12,254

correct answer: _____

16.   7864
      + 1155   − _____
       9919

correct answer: _____

Check these addition problems by adding again in a different order.
Write the correct answer for each problem.

17. 11,012   6,498
      + 6,498   + _____
      17,500

correct answer: _____

18.   4831
      +3070   + _____
       7801

correct answer: _____

Name _____ Date _____

Arrange the numbers in a column and add.   124

19. 27, 15, 83   **20.** 156, 18, 50   **21.** 237, 481, 725   **22.** 1024, 256, 16, 4

Add the decimals.   125

23. 1.7   **24.** 17.4   **25.** 15.02   **26.** 108.7   **27.** 15.086   **28.** 219.23
  +3.3   +20.8   +30.28   24.2   21.932   114.87
                                                 + 31.6   +6.025   +150.77

Face painting	$46.35
Baked goods	$83.75
Crafts	$34.16
Food	$109.27
Drinks	$64.30

The students at South Street School held a fair to raise money. The table shows how much money was made at each tent.

29. How much money did the students raise?

_____

Arrange the decimals in a column and add.   125-126

30. 27.2, 108.4, 6.3   **31.** 15.76, 20.1, 125.5   **32.** 190.5, 90.07, 218.41

33. 12.186, 10.605, 11.07, 15.256   **34.** 0.415, 0.7, 1.02, 0.873

Name _____ Date _____

Addition

Directions: Compute. Mark the letter beside the answer to each problem.

1. 127
    +64

    A 181
    B 190
    C 191
    D 192

2. 325
    +409

    E 724
    F 734
    G 725
    H 735

3.   98
    1376
    +815

    A 1289
    B 2179
    C 2189
    D 2289

4. 5.29
    +1.73

    E 7.92
    F 7.02
    G 6.92
    H 6.02

5. 2.26
    0.15
    +9.34

    A 10.75
    B 10.85
    C 11.75
    D 11.85

Directions: Solve each problem. Write your answer.

6. At the Ames School, 114 students are girls and 98 are boys. How many students are there in all?

    _____

7. Nina played a video game and got scores of 173, 255, and 194. What was her total score?

    _____

8. A bricklayer used 1155 bricks to build a chimney and 682 bricks to build a walk. How many bricks were used in all?

    _____

9. Ramon made three long jumps of 2.7 meters, 3.15 meters, and 4.62 meters. What was the total length of his three jumps?

    _____

10. Shana bought a sweatshirt for $19.95 and running shoes for $59.50. Including a tax of $3.97, what was the total cost?

    _____

PRACTICE ANSWERS
Page 44

1. 289
2. 925
3. 2496
4. 8219
5. 343
6. 4411
7. 1113
8. 13,619
9. 10,005
10. 51,011
11. 6921
12. 92,302

For questions 13–16, students may subtract either addend.

13. correct answer: 515
14. correct answer: 4822
15. correct answer: 13,254
16. correct answer: 9019
17. correct answer: 17,510
18. correct answer: 7901

Page 45

19. 125
20. 224
21. 1443
22. 1300
23. 5.0
24. 38.2
25. 45.30
26. 164.5
27. 43.043
28. 484.87
29. $337.83
30. 141.9
31. 161.36
32. 498.98
33. 49.117
34. 3.008

TEST PREP ANSWERS
Page 46

1. C
2. F
3. D
4. F
5. C
6. 212 students
7. 622
8. 1837 bricks
9. 10.47 m
10. $83.42

Name _____ Date _____

Subtraction

129-130 Rewrite and solve each problem. Be sure to line up the digits by place value.

1. 84 − 21   **2.** 163 − 12   **3.** 478 − 235   **4.** 7318 − 2107

_____   _____   _____   _____

130-132 Solve each problem.

5.   333   **6.**   758   **7.**   8096   **8.**   11,425
        −205   −294   −450   −1,012

9.   2149   **10.** 36,489   **11.** 50,397   **12.** 63,428
       − 1345   −8,250   −40,289   −42,106

13. 116,450   **14.**   4071   **15.** 23,677   **16.** 325,016
       −17,504   −888   −12,601   −275,545

133 Subtract.

17.   117   **18.**   5012   **19.**   2814   **20.** 10,000
          −99   − 28   −2783   − 1,876

21.   5956   **22.** 32,016   **23.**   8425   **24.** 73,906
         −789   −29,408   −6729   −64,898

Name _____ Date _____

Use addition to check these subtraction problems.
Write the correct answer for each problem.

134

25. 6395   2915
  − 4480   + _____
  2915
  correct answer: _____

26. 847
  − 379   + _____
  468
  correct answer: _____

27. 13,024
  −7,260   + _____
  5,864
  correct answer: _____

28. 469,720
  −125,650   + _____
  344,170
  correct answer: _____

Rewrite and solve each problem.

135

29. $14.7 - 3.8$ **30.** $0.86 - 0.23$ **31.** $125.7 - 63.73$ **32.** $41.85 - 39.08$

_____   _____   _____   _____

Subtract the decimals.

33. 23.984
  − 16.009

34. 4.71
  −0.98

35. 160.234
  −47.301

36. 2.76
  − 1.08

37. 1367.6
  − 75.8

38. 14.846
  −12.907

39. 5.005
  − 3.250

40. 29.86
  −21.77

41. You have $32.00. You buy a jacket for $29.95
plus $0.90 tax. How much money do you have left? _____

132, 135

42. From Gary, Indiana, it is 260 miles to Terre Haute and 184 miles
to Muncie. How much farther is Terre Haute from Gary than Muncie? _____

43. Today the outside temperature is 81°F.
Yesterday it was 12° colder. What was the temperature yesterday? _____

Name _____ Date _____

Subtraction

Directions: Solve each problem. Fill in the circle beside your answer.

1.   345
    − 72

○ **A.**   253

○ **B.**   263

○ **C.**   273

2.   4029
    − 750

○ **A.**   3269

○ **B.**   3279

○ **C.**   3379

3. 786 − 277 =

○ **A.**   509

○ **B.**   518

○ **C.**   519

4. 6.54 − 3.98 =

○ **A.**   2.66

○ **B.**   2.56

○ **C.**   2.44

5. $10.25 − $1.95 =

○ **A.** $7.30

○ **B.** $8.20

○ **C.** $8.30

6. There are 365 days in a year. If this is the 208th day, how many days are left?

○ **A.**   257

○ **B.**   163

○ **C.**   157

7. Garth bought groceries for $41.73. He gave the clerk $50.00. How much change should he receive?

○ **A.** $9.27

○ **B.** $8.27

○ **C.** $8.17

8. Glen Curtis was born on January 10, 1937. How old was he on January 10, 2000?

○ **A.**   63 years old

○ **B.**   64 years old

○ **C.**   73 years old

9. Joni ran 40 yards in 7.08 seconds. Maggie ran 40 yards in 6.25 seconds. How much faster was Maggie's time?

○ **A.**   1.17 seconds

○ **B.**   0.93 seconds

○ **C.**   0.83 seconds

PRACTICE ANSWERS
Page 48
1. 63
2. 151
3. 243
4. 5211
5. 128
6. 464
7. 7646
8. 10,413
9. 804
10. 28,239
11. 10,108
12. 21,322
13. 98,946
14. 3183
15. 11,076
16. 49,471
17. 18
18. 4984
19. 31
20. 8124
21. 5167
22. 2608
23. 1696
24. 9008

Page 49
25. correct answer: 1915
26. correct answer: 468
27. correct answer: 5764
28. correct answer: 344,070
29. 10.9
30. 0.63
31. 61.97
32. 2.77
33. 7.975
34. 3.73
35. 112.933
36. 1.68
37. 1291.8
38. 1.939
39. 1.755
40. 8.09
41. $1.15
42. 76 miles
43. 69°F

TEST PREP ANSWERS
Page 50
1. C
2. B
3. A
4. B
5. C
6. C
7. B
8. A
9. C

Name _____ Date _____

Multiplication

ONE WAY Multiply. List all the partial products and add.

```
H  T  O
2  1  5
×     3
   1  5  ← Multiply the ones.
   3  0  ← Multiply the tens.
6  0  0  ← Multiply the hundreds.
6  4  5  ← Add the partial products.
```

ANOTHER WAY Multiply without listing the partial products.

```
   H  T  O
   1  1
   2  3  3
×        6
1  3  9  8  ← Multiply the ones.
            ─── Multiply the tens.
            ─── Multiply the hundreds.
```

138-140 Multiply. Use the way that works best for you.

1. 153
    × 4

2. 437
    × 8

3. 178
    × 7

4. 525
    × 5

5. 723
    × 3

6. 151
    × 9

7. 635
    × 2

8. 210
    × 3

9. 823
    × 6

10. 458
    × 5

11. 78
    ×33

12. 26
    ×51

13. 32
    ×25

14. 81
    ×17

15. 63
    ×72

16. 15
    ×43

17. 48
    ×31

18. 50
    ×64

19. 29
    ×40

20. 72
    ×12

Name _____ Date _____

Check these products. If the answer is correct, circle *correct*.
If the answer is incorrect, circle *incorrect* and write the correct product.

141

21.   88
   ×27
  2276

22.   73
   ×55
  4015

23.   15
   ×27
   505

correct incorrect: _____

correct incorrect: _____

correct incorrect: _____

Place the decimal point in each product.

143

24.   1.7
  ×2.3
  391

25.   14.3
  × 6.5
  9295

26.   10.02
  × 7.25
 726450

27. 3.005
  × 1.9
 57095

28.   7.1
  ×13.6
 9656

Multiply the decimals.

142-143

29. 15.82
  × 2.5

30. 150.5
  × 4.8

31. 81.2
  × 0.5

32. 27.84
  × 5.9

33. 15.4
  ×0.07

Show your work for each of these problems.

34. One can of soup costs $0.67. How much will 6 cans cost? _____

35. Sam walks 1.3 miles one way to school every day. How many miles
will he walk if he makes five round trips between home and school? _____

36. Each panel in a quilt is made using 13 pieces of cloth.
How many pieces of cloth are there in a quilt with 25 panels? _____

Name _____ Date _____

Multiplication

Directions: Solve each problem. Mark the letter beside your answer.

1 $125 \times 9 =$

- A   1025
- B   1115
- C   1125
- D   1225

2 $11 \times 36 =$

- F   361
- G   366
- H   386
- J   396

3 $27 \times 50 =$

- A   450
- B   1,350
- C   1,450
- D   13,500

4 $0.08 \times 0.2 =$

- F   0.016
- G   0.16
- H   1.60
- J   16.0

5 $2.39 \times 0.5 =$

- A   11.95
- B   11.55
- C   1.195
- D   1.55

6 Mr. James works 45 hours per week. How many hours will he work in 12 weeks?

- F   550 hr
- G   540 hr
- H   530 hr
- J   440 hr

7 A kitchen floor has 14 rows of tiles with 28 tiles in each row. How many tiles are there in all?

- A   392 tiles
- B   382 tiles
- C   292 tiles
- D   284 tiles

8 Kent bought 6.8 feet of molding at $0.90 per foot. What was the total cost of the molding?

- F $6.22
- G $6.12
- H $6.02
- J $0.61

9 The power company charges $0.75 per unit of electricity. What is the charge for 0.4 units?

- A $0.03
- B $0.28
- C $0.30
- D $3.00

PRACTICE ANSWERS
Page 52

1. 612
2. 3496
3. 1246
4. 2625
5. 2169
6. 1359
7. 1270
8. 630
9. 4938
10. 2290
11. 2574
12. 1326
13. 800
14. 1377
15. 4536
16. 645
17. 1488
18. 3200
19. 1160
20. 864

Page 53

21. incorrect: 2376
22. correct
23. incorrect: 405
24. 3.91
25. 92.95
26. 72.6450
27. 5.7095
28. 96.56
29. 39.55
30. 722.40
31. 40.60
32. 164.256
33. 1.078
34. $4.02
35. 13 miles
36. 325

TEST PREP ANSWERS
Page 54

1. C
2. J
3. B
4. F
5. C
6. G
7. A
8. G
9. C

Name _____ Date _____

Division

146-147 Solve each problem. Show your work.

1. $3\overline{)45}$ **2.** $7\overline{)84}$ **3.** $5\overline{)320}$ **4.** $2\overline{)146}$ **5.** $6\overline{)90}$

6. $9\overline{)243}$ **7.** $4\overline{)160}$ **8.** $6\overline{)102}$ **9.** $8\overline{)176}$ **10.** $7\overline{)133}$

Rewrite and solve each problem. Show your work.

11. $24 \div 3$ **12.** $105 \div 7$ **13.** $96 \div 4$ **14.** $135 \div 9$ **15.** $648 \div 8$

148 Solve each problem.

16. $2\overline{)83}$ R   **17.** $7\overline{)101}$ R   **18.** $4\overline{)47}$ R   **19.** $8\overline{)185}$ R   **20.** $5\overline{)511}$ R

21. $8\overline{)90}$ R   **22.** $9\overline{)285}$ R   **23.** $3\overline{)205}$ R   **24.** $6\overline{)99}$ R   **25.** $10\overline{)635}$ R

148-149 Solve each problem. Write the remainders as fractions in simplest form.

26. $6\overline{)57}$ **27.** $3\overline{)124}$ **28.** $8\overline{)126}$ **29.** $7\overline{)176}$ **30.** $4\overline{)209}$

Name _____ Date _____

Solve each problem. For each one, tell how you interpret the remainder.

149

31. The Snells are expecting 44 people to attend their annual reunion. They plan to rent tables that seat 8 people. How many tables will they need?

_____

32. You are sharing 4 dozen cookies among 5 friends. How many cookies will you have left over? _____

33. How many two-foot lengths can be cut from an eleven-foot piece of lumber? _____

_____

Solve each division problem. Then write and solve a multiplication problem to check your division. Remember to add remainders to the product when checking your work.

152

34. $7\overline{)760}$

$$\times \quad 7$$

35. $9\overline{)456}$

$$\times \quad $$

Solve each problem. Show your work.

153-155

36. $2\overline{)15.8}$ **37.** $1.2\overline{)60}$ **38.** $0.5\overline{)17}$ **39.** $50\overline{)24}$

40. $7\overline{)28.7}$ **41.** $0.65\overline{)325}$ **42.** $80\overline{)40}$ **43.** $1.5\overline{)135}$

Name _____ Date _____

Division

Directions: Solve each problem. Mark the letter for your answer.
If your answer is not given, mark "None of these."

1 320 ÷ 4 =
- **A**   8
- **B**   78
- **C**   80
- **D**   82
- **E**   None of these

2 58 ÷ 9 =
- **F**   6
- **G**   6 R4
- **H**   6 R6
- **J**   7 R2
- **K**   None of these

3 7)743
- **A**   16
- **B**   16 R1
- **C**   106
- **D**   106 R3
- **E**   None of these

4 $21.57 ÷ 3 =
- **F** $6.19
- **G** $7.09
- **H** $7.19
- **J** $7.29
- **K**   None of these

5 Yoshi stacked 78 books in 6 equal piles. How many books were in each pile?
- **A**   12   **C**   14
- **B**   13   **D**   16

6 Mrs. Kline had 420 stickers. She gave an equal number of stickers to each of 60 students. How many stickers did each student get?
- **F**   7   **H**   70
- **G**   8   **J**   80

7 An ant is 0.25 inches long. How many ants would be needed to make a line of ants 15 inches long?
- **A**   14   **C**   40
- **B**   30   **D**   60

8 Three girls earned a total of $81.48 at a tag sale. If the 3 girls divide the money equally, how much will each girl receive?
- **F** $27.06   **H** $27.16
- **G** $27.12   **J** $40.74

PRACTICE ANSWERS
Page 56

1. 15
2. 12
3. 64
4. 73
5. 15
6. 27
7. 40
8. 17
9. 22
10. 19
11. 8
12. 15
13. 24
14. 15
15. 81
16. 41 R1
17. 14 R3
18. 11 R3
19. 23 R1
20. 102 R1
21. 11 R2
22. 31 R6
23. 68 R1
24. 16 R3
25. 63 R5
26. $9\frac{1}{2}$
27. $41\frac{1}{3}$
28. $15\frac{3}{4}$
29. $25\frac{1}{7}$
30. $52\frac{1}{4}$

Page 57

31. 6 tables.
    $44 \div 8 = 5$ R4. The answer is the next greater number.
32. 3 cookies.
    $48 \div 5 = 9$ R3. Use the remainder as the answer.
33. 5. $11 \div 2 = 5$ R1. Ignore the remainder.
34. 108 R4;
    $(108 \times 7) + 4 = 760$
35. 50 R6; $(50 \times 9) + 6 = 456$
36. 7.9
37. 50
38. 34
39. 0.48
40. 4.1
41. 500
42. 0.5
43. 90

TEST PREP ANSWERS
Page 58

1. C
2. G
3. E
4. H
5. B
6. F
7. D
8. H

Back to School

TIME
• 45–60 minutes

OBJECTIVES
- Add and multiply money amounts
- Use reasonableness to select decimal numbers to add and multiply

MATERIALS
- Math Notebook Page, page 190
- calculators (optional)

TEACHER NOTES
- This activity will give students practice adding and multiplying decimals. As they try to reach certain dollar amounts, they should see that multiplying the cost by the quantity is quicker than adding the cost of duplicate items.

- Suggest that the students use an organized list to solve the last problem.

EXTENSIONS
- Use a real ad and have the students try to make purchases totaling a given amount.

- Have the students estimate the cost of various quantities of an item. This will give the students practice using mental math and estimation skills with dollar amounts.

ANSWERS
1. Check student estimates. The total cost of one of each item is $6.36. Students should quickly see that the cost will be more than $5.00, since the cost of the four most expensive items is very close to that amount.

2. Pencils: 2 dozen

3. Highlighters: 1

4. Glue: 6

5. Pens: 2 boxes

6. Crayons: 3 boxes

7. Filler Paper: 20 packages

8. Theme Books: 4

9. Folders: 37

10. Answers will vary. Check student work for accuracy.

11. Here is one possible solution.

Item	Quantity	Cost	Total
Pencils	1	$1.29	$1.29
Highlighters	1	$1.59	$1.59
School Glue	6	$0.48	$2.88
Pens	1	$1.09	$1.09
Crayons	1	$0.99	$0.99
Filler Paper	2	$0.15	$0.30
Theme Books	2	$0.69	$1.38
Solid-color Folders	6	$0.08	$0.48
TOTAL	20		$10.00

Name _____ Date _____

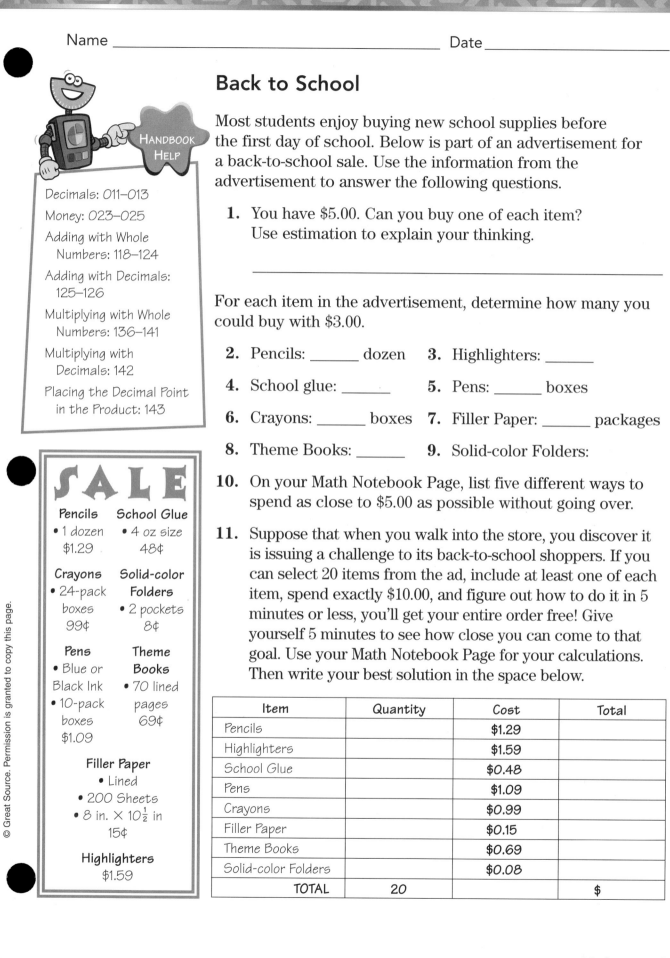

HANDBOOK HELP

Decimals: 011–013

Money: 023–025

Adding with Whole Numbers: 118–124

Adding with Decimals: 125–126

Multiplying with Whole Numbers: 136–141

Multiplying with Decimals: 142

Placing the Decimal Point in the Product: 143

Back to School

Most students enjoy buying new school supplies before the first day of school. Below is part of an advertisement for a back-to-school sale. Use the information from the advertisement to answer the following questions.

1. You have $5.00. Can you buy one of each item? Use estimation to explain your thinking.

_____

For each item in the advertisement, determine how many you could buy with $3.00.

2. Pencils: _____ dozen   3. Highlighters: _____

4. School glue: _____   5. Pens: _____ boxes

6. Crayons: _____ boxes   7. Filler Paper: _____ packages

8. Theme Books: _____   9. Solid-color Folders:

10. On your Math Notebook Page, list five different ways to spend as close to $5.00 as possible without going over.

11. Suppose that when you walk into the store, you discover it is issuing a challenge to its back-to-school shoppers. If you can select 20 items from the ad, include at least one of each item, spend exactly $10.00, and figure out how to do it in 5 minutes or less, you'll get your entire order free! Give yourself 5 minutes to see how close you can come to that goal. Use your Math Notebook Page for your calculations. Then write your best solution in the space below.

SALE

Pencils
• 1 dozen
$1.29

School Glue
• 4 oz size
48¢

Crayons
• 24-pack boxes
99¢

Solid-color Folders
• 2 pockets
8¢

Pens
• Blue or Black Ink
• 10-pack boxes
$1.09

Theme Books
• 70 lined pages
69¢

Filler Paper
• Lined
• 200 Sheets
• 8 in. × 10½ in
15¢

Highlighters
$1.59

Item	Quantity	Cost	Total
Pencils		$1.29	
Highlighters		$1.59	
School Glue		$0.48	
Pens		$1.09	
Crayons		$0.99	
Filler Paper		$0.15	
Theme Books		$0.69	
Solid-color Folders		$0.08	
TOTAL	20		$

Name _____ Date _____

Adding with Fractions

Add: $\frac{5}{8} + \frac{1}{8}$

ONE WAY Think of a number line divided into eighths. It will still be divided into eighths after adding. The denominator stays the same.

$$\frac{5}{8} \qquad \frac{1}{8}$$

$$0 \qquad\qquad \frac{6}{8} \text{ or } \frac{3}{4} \qquad 1$$

ANOTHER WAY

Check that the denominators are the same. Use that denominator in the sum.	Add the numerators.	Simplify if possible.
$\frac{5}{8} + \frac{1}{8} = \frac{}{8}$	$\frac{5}{8} + \frac{1}{8} = \frac{6}{8}$	$6 \div 2 = \frac{3}{4}$

Add: $\frac{7}{12} + \frac{7}{12}$

Use the same denominator.	Add the numerators.	Simplify and regroup.
$\frac{7}{12} + \frac{7}{12} = \frac{}{12}$	$\frac{7}{12} + \frac{7}{12} = \frac{14}{12}$	$14 \div 2 = \frac{7}{6} = 1\frac{1}{6}$

158-159 Add the fractions. Write your answer in simplest form.

1. $\frac{2}{5} + \frac{1}{5} =$ _____

2. $\frac{3}{8} + \frac{1}{8} =$ _____

3. $\frac{2}{7} + \frac{4}{7} =$ _____

4. $\frac{1}{6} + \frac{1}{6} =$ _____

5. $\frac{1}{12} + \frac{7}{12} =$ _____

6. $\frac{3}{10} + \frac{3}{10} =$ _____

7. $\frac{5}{8} + \frac{3}{8} =$ _____

8. $\frac{5}{6} + \frac{5}{6} =$ _____

9. $\frac{3}{5} + \frac{4}{5} =$ _____

10. $\frac{3}{4} + \frac{3}{4} =$ _____

11. $\frac{7}{10} + \frac{9}{10} =$ _____

12. $\frac{7}{12} + \frac{11}{12} =$ _____

13. $\frac{3}{16} + \frac{9}{16} =$ _____

14. $\frac{4}{15} + \frac{8}{15} =$ _____

15. $\frac{11}{20} + \frac{13}{20} =$ _____

159 Add and then compare the fractions. Write >, <, or = in each blank.

$\frac{3}{10} + \frac{1}{10} \underline{\leq} \frac{1}{2}$ The sum is $\frac{4}{10}$, which is less than $\frac{5}{10}$, or $\frac{1}{2}$. Write <.

16. $\frac{7}{12} + \frac{1}{12}$ _____ $\frac{2}{3}$

17. $\frac{3}{8} + \frac{3}{8}$ _____ 1

18. $\frac{5}{16} + \frac{7}{16}$ _____ $\frac{5}{8}$

19. $\frac{7}{20} + \frac{9}{20}$ _____ $\frac{3}{4}$

20. $\frac{3}{5} + \frac{3}{5}$ _____ 1

21. $\frac{3}{14} + \frac{5}{14}$ _____ $\frac{5}{7}$

Name _____ Date _____

Add: $\frac{1}{2} + \frac{1}{3}$

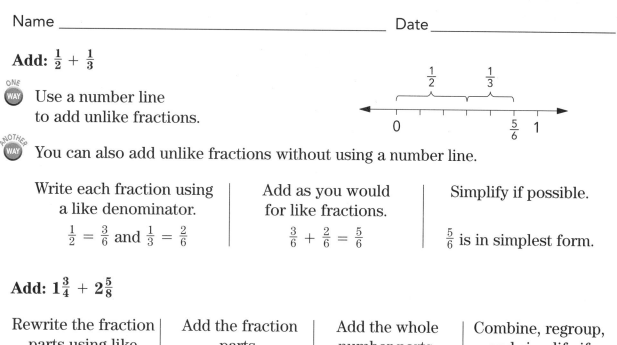

ONE WAY Use a number line to add unlike fractions.

ANOTHER WAY You can also add unlike fractions without using a number line.

Write each fraction using a like denominator.	Add as you would for like fractions.	Simplify if possible.
$\frac{1}{2} = \frac{3}{6}$ and $\frac{1}{3} = \frac{2}{6}$	$\frac{3}{6} + \frac{2}{6} = \frac{5}{6}$	$\frac{5}{6}$ is in simplest form.

Add: $1\frac{3}{4} + 2\frac{5}{8}$

Rewrite the fraction parts using like denominators.	Add the fraction parts.	Add the whole number parts.	Combine, regroup, and simplify if possible.
$\frac{3}{4} = \frac{6}{8}$ and $\frac{5}{8} = \frac{5}{8}$	$\frac{6}{8} + \frac{5}{8} = \frac{11}{8}$	$1 + 2 = 3$	$3\frac{11}{8} =$ $3 + \frac{8}{8} + \frac{3}{8} = 4\frac{3}{8}$

Rewrite each sum using like denominators. Then add.

$\frac{1}{2} + \frac{2}{7} \longrightarrow \frac{7}{14} + \frac{4}{14} = \frac{11}{14}$

160-161

22. $\frac{2}{5} + \frac{3}{10} \longrightarrow$ _____ + _____ = _____

23. $\frac{2}{3} + \frac{1}{6} \longrightarrow$ _____ + _____ = _____

24. $\frac{1}{2} + \frac{7}{10} \longrightarrow$ _____ + _____ = _____

25. $\frac{2}{3} + \frac{1}{4} \longrightarrow$ _____ + _____ = _____

26. $2\frac{2}{3} + \frac{5}{8} \longrightarrow$ _____ + _____ = _____

27. $3\frac{4}{5} + 2\frac{2}{3} \longrightarrow$ _____ + _____ = _____

28. $4\frac{1}{6} + 1\frac{3}{4} \longrightarrow$ _____ + _____ = _____

29. $5\frac{3}{4} + \frac{7}{10} \longrightarrow$ _____ + _____ = _____

Name _____ Date _____

Adding with Fractions

Directions: Mark the letter beside the best answer to each question.

1. Shem and Margo shared a pizza. Shem ate $\frac{3}{8}$ and Margo ate $\frac{1}{4}$. How much did they eat in all?

   A. $\frac{4}{8}$

   B. $\frac{1}{2}$

   C. $\frac{5}{8}$

   D. $\frac{3}{4}$

2. Sally mixed $\frac{1}{2}$ gallon of water and $\frac{3}{10}$ gallon of fruit juice in a one-gallon pot. How full is the pot?

   A. $\frac{3}{5}$

   B. $\frac{7}{10}$

   C. $\frac{2}{3}$

   D. $\frac{4}{5}$

3. Henry walked $2\frac{1}{2}$ miles on Monday and $1\frac{1}{4}$ miles on Tuesday. How far did he walk in all?

   A. $3\frac{1}{8}$ miles

   B. $3\frac{1}{4}$ miles

   C. $3\frac{3}{4}$ miles

   D. $3\frac{7}{8}$ miles

4. Doris read $\frac{1}{6}$ of a book one day and $\frac{2}{3}$ of the book the next day. How much of the book did she read in 2 days?

   A. $\frac{5}{6}$

   B. $\frac{1}{2}$

   C. $\frac{3}{6}$

   D. $\frac{3}{9}$

5. Honus put $\frac{3}{4}$ of a cup of brown sugar and $\frac{2}{3}$ of a cup of white sugar in a pan. How much sugar was in the pan?

   A. $\frac{5}{7}$ of a cup

   B. $1\frac{1}{4}$ cups

   C. $1\frac{1}{3}$ cups

   D. $1\frac{5}{12}$ cups

6. Melanie rode $1\frac{1}{2}$ miles on her bike and then walked $\frac{6}{10}$ of a mile. How far did she travel in all?

   A. $1\frac{7}{12}$ miles

   B. $2\frac{1}{10}$ miles

   C. $2\frac{1}{4}$ miles

   D. $2\frac{7}{10}$ miles

PRACTICE ANSWERS
Page 62

1. $\frac{3}{5}$

2. $\frac{1}{2}$

3. $\frac{6}{7}$

4. $\frac{1}{3}$

5. $\frac{2}{3}$

6. $\frac{3}{5}$

7. 1

8. $1\frac{2}{3}$

9. $1\frac{2}{5}$

10. $1\frac{1}{2}$

11. $1\frac{3}{5}$

12. $1\frac{1}{2}$

13. $\frac{3}{4}$

14. $\frac{4}{5}$

15. $1\frac{1}{5}$

16. $\frac{2}{3} = \frac{2}{3}$

17. $\frac{3}{4} < 1$

18. $\frac{3}{4} > \frac{5}{8}$

19. $\frac{4}{5} > \frac{3}{4}$

20. $1\frac{1}{5} > 1$

21. $\frac{4}{7} < \frac{5}{7}$

Page 63

22. $\frac{4}{10} + \frac{3}{10} = \frac{7}{10}$

23. $\frac{4}{6} + \frac{1}{6} = \frac{5}{6}$

24. $\frac{5}{10} + \frac{7}{10} = 1\frac{1}{5}$

25. $\frac{8}{12} + \frac{3}{12} = \frac{11}{12}$

26. $2\frac{16}{24} + \frac{15}{24} = 3\frac{7}{24}$

27. $3\frac{12}{15} + 2\frac{10}{15} = 6\frac{7}{15}$

28. $4\frac{2}{12} + 1\frac{9}{12} = 5\frac{11}{12}$

29. $5\frac{15}{20} + \frac{14}{20} = 6\frac{9}{20}$

TEST PREP ANSWERS
Page 64

1. C

2. D

3. C

4. A

5. D

6. B

Name _____ Date _____

Subtracting with Fractions

Subtract: $\frac{5}{6} - \frac{1}{6}$

ONE WAY Think of a number line divided into sixths.
It will still be divided into sixths after subtracting.
The denominator stays the same.

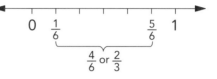

ANOTHER WAY You can subtract without using a number line.

Check that the denominators are the same.	Subtract the numerators. Use the same denominator.	Regroup and simplify if possible.
In $\frac{5}{6} - \frac{1}{6}$, they are both 6.	$\frac{5}{6} - \frac{1}{6} = \frac{4}{6}$	$\frac{4}{6} \longrightarrow \frac{4 \div 2}{6 \div 2} = \frac{2}{3}$

Subtract: $2 - \frac{2}{3}$

Regroup the whole number using the same denominator as the fraction.	Subtract the numerators, since the fractions have the same denominator.	Regroup and simplify if possible.
$2 = \frac{6}{3}$	$\frac{6}{3} - \frac{2}{3} = \frac{4}{3}$	$\frac{4}{3} \longrightarrow \frac{3}{3} + \frac{1}{3} = 1\frac{1}{3}$

163-164 Subtract the fractions. Write your answer in simplest form.

1. $\frac{4}{5} - \frac{2}{5} =$ _____   2. $\frac{7}{9} - \frac{1}{9} =$ _____   3. $\frac{5}{8} - \frac{2}{8} =$ _____

4. $\frac{9}{10} - \frac{7}{10} =$ _____   5. $\frac{5}{7} - \frac{4}{7} =$ _____   6. $\frac{11}{12} - \frac{7}{12} =$ _____

7. $1 - \frac{5}{8} =$ _____   8. $1 - \frac{9}{10} =$ _____   9. $1 - \frac{7}{9} =$ _____

10. $2 - \frac{3}{5} =$ _____   11. $4 - \frac{1}{6} =$ _____   12. $3 - \frac{7}{8} =$ _____

13. $\frac{2}{3} - \frac{1}{3} =$ _____   14. $\frac{11}{16} - \frac{7}{16} =$ _____   15. $2 - \frac{2}{5} =$ _____

Subtract and then compare the fractions. Write >, <, or = in each blank.

$\frac{5}{6} - \frac{2}{6} \geq \frac{1}{3}$ The difference is $\frac{3}{6}$ or $\frac{1}{2}$, which is more than $\frac{1}{3}$. Write >.

16. $2 - \frac{7}{8}$ _____ 1   17. $\frac{11}{12} - \frac{8}{12}$ _____ $\frac{1}{4}$ 18. $\frac{15}{16} - \frac{9}{16}$ _____ $\frac{1}{2}$

Name _____ Date _____

To subtract fractions with unlike denominators, first rewrite
the fractions using like denominators. You may need to regroup
a mixed number before you subtract.

Subtract: $\frac{3}{4} - \frac{1}{3}$

Rewrite the fractions using like denominators.	Subtract the numerators, since the fractions have the same denominator.	Write the difference in simplest form.
$\frac{3}{4} = \frac{9}{12}$ and $\frac{1}{3} = \frac{4}{12}$	$\frac{9}{12} - \frac{4}{12} = \frac{5}{12}$	$\frac{5}{12}$ is in simplest form.

Subtract: $1\frac{1}{2} - \frac{5}{6}$

Rewrite the fractions using like denominators.	Regroup and subtract.	Simplify if possible.
$1\frac{1}{2} = 1\frac{3}{6}$ and $\frac{5}{6} = \frac{5}{6}$	$1\frac{3}{6} - \frac{5}{6} = \frac{9}{6} - \frac{5}{6} = \frac{4}{6}$	$\frac{4}{6} \longrightarrow \frac{4 \div 2}{6 \div 2} = \frac{2}{3}$

Rewrite each difference using common denominators. Then subtract.   165-166

19. $\frac{7}{12} - \frac{1}{6} =$ _____ $-$ _____ $=$ _____   **20.** $\frac{13}{16} - \frac{1}{2} =$ _____ $-$ _____ $=$ _____

21. $\frac{2}{3} - \frac{1}{12} =$ _____ $-$ _____ $=$ _____   **22.** $\frac{3}{4} - \frac{2}{3} =$ _____ $-$ _____ $=$ _____

23. $\frac{4}{5} - \frac{1}{2} =$ _____ $-$ _____ $=$ _____   **24.** $\frac{7}{10} - \frac{1}{3} =$ _____ $-$ _____ $=$ _____

25. $\frac{3}{4} - \frac{1}{6} =$ _____ $-$ _____ $=$ _____   **26.** $\frac{3}{4} - \frac{3}{10} =$ _____ $-$ _____ $=$ _____

27. $\frac{5}{6} - \frac{3}{8} =$ _____ $-$ _____ $=$ _____   **28.** $1\frac{3}{4} - \frac{1}{8} =$ _____ $-$ _____ $=$ _____

29. $1\frac{2}{3} - \frac{1}{2} =$ _____ $-$ _____ $=$ _____   **30.** $2\frac{4}{5} - \frac{7}{10} =$ _____ $-$ _____ $=$ _____

31. $1\frac{7}{8} - \frac{15}{16} =$ _____ $-$ _____ $=$ _____   **32.** $3\frac{5}{8} - \frac{4}{5} =$ _____ $-$ _____ $=$ _____

33. $2\frac{1}{6} \longrightarrow$ _____   **34.** $8\frac{2}{3} \longrightarrow$ _____   **35.** $5\frac{3}{8} \longrightarrow$ _____

   $- 1\frac{7}{10} \longrightarrow$ _____ $- 5\frac{1}{2} \longrightarrow -$ _____ $- 1\frac{3}{4} \longrightarrow -$ _____

Name _____ Date _____

Subtracting with Fractions

Directions: Mark the letter of the best answer to each question.

1. Theo jogged $\frac{7}{8}$ of a mile. Nan jogged $\frac{3}{4}$ of a mile. How much farther did Theo jog?

   A. $\frac{1}{8}$ mile

   B. $\frac{1}{3}$ mile

   C. $\frac{1}{4}$ mile

   D. $\frac{3}{8}$ mile

2. Pam mowed her lawn in $1\frac{1}{2}$ hours, and Kate mowed hers in $2\frac{1}{4}$ hours. How much less time did Pam's lawn take?

   A. $\frac{1}{2}$ hr

   B. $\frac{1}{4}$ hr

   C. $\frac{2}{3}$ hr

   D. $\frac{3}{4}$ hr

3. Steve had $1\frac{3}{4}$ quarts of lemonade. He drank $\frac{2}{3}$ of a quart. How much did he have left?

   A. $1\frac{1}{4}$ qt

   B. $1\frac{1}{2}$ qt

   C. $1\frac{1}{12}$ qt

   D. $1\frac{1}{3}$ qt

Directions: Solve each problem. Write your answer.

4. Andy and Ray bought a loaf of bread. Andy ate $\frac{1}{3}$ of the loaf and Ray ate $\frac{3}{8}$. Who ate more bread, Andy or Ray? Explain.

5. Doty had $\frac{9}{10}$ of a gallon of milk. She used $\frac{1}{2}$ gallon to make milk shakes. How much milk was left? (Show your work.)

6. Lamont swam $5\frac{1}{2}$ laps in the swimming pool. Earl swam $4\frac{1}{6}$ laps. How much farther did Lamont swim? (Show your work.)

PRACTICE ANSWERS
Page 66

1. $\frac{2}{5}$

2. $\frac{2}{3}$

3. $\frac{3}{8}$

4. $\frac{1}{5}$

5. $\frac{1}{7}$

6. $\frac{1}{3}$

7. $\frac{3}{8}$

8. $\frac{1}{10}$

9. $\frac{2}{9}$

10. $1\frac{2}{5}$

11. $3\frac{5}{6}$

12. $2\frac{1}{8}$

13. $\frac{1}{3}$

14. $\frac{1}{4}$

15. $1\frac{3}{5}$

16. $1\frac{1}{8} > 1$

17. $\frac{1}{4} = \frac{1}{4}$

18. $\frac{3}{8} < \frac{1}{2}$

Page 67

19. $\frac{7}{12} - \frac{2}{12} = \frac{5}{12}$

20. $\frac{13}{16} - \frac{8}{16} = \frac{5}{16}$

21. $\frac{8}{12} - \frac{1}{12} = \frac{7}{12}$

22. $\frac{9}{12} - \frac{8}{12} = \frac{1}{12}$

23. $\frac{8}{10} - \frac{5}{10} = \frac{3}{10}$

24. $\frac{21}{30} - \frac{10}{30} = \frac{11}{30}$

25. $\frac{9}{12} - \frac{2}{12} = \frac{7}{12}$

26. $\frac{15}{20} - \frac{6}{20} = \frac{9}{20}$

27. $\frac{20}{24} - \frac{9}{24} = \frac{11}{24}$

28. $1\frac{6}{8} - \frac{1}{8} = 1\frac{5}{8}$

29. $1\frac{4}{6} - \frac{3}{6} = 1\frac{1}{6}$

30. $2\frac{8}{10} - \frac{7}{10} = 2\frac{1}{10}$

31. $\frac{30}{16} - \frac{15}{16} = \frac{15}{16}$

32. $2\frac{65}{40} - \frac{32}{40} = 2\frac{33}{40}$

33. $1\frac{35}{30} - 1\frac{21}{30} = \frac{7}{15}$

34. $8\frac{4}{6} - 5\frac{3}{6} = 3\frac{1}{6}$

35. $4\frac{11}{8} - 1\frac{6}{8} = 3\frac{5}{8}$

TEST PREP ANSWERS
Page 68

1. A

2. D

3. C

4. Ray ate more. Andy ate $\frac{1}{3}$, or $\frac{8}{24}$. Ray ate $\frac{3}{8}$, or $\frac{9}{24}$.

5. $\frac{2}{5}$ gal. ($\frac{1}{2} = \frac{5}{10}$ gal; $\frac{9}{10} - \frac{5}{10} = \frac{4}{10}$, or $\frac{2}{5}$)

6. $1\frac{1}{3}$ laps. ($5\frac{1}{2} = \frac{11}{2} = \frac{33}{6}$; $4\frac{1}{6} = \frac{25}{6}$; $\frac{33}{6} - \frac{25}{6} = \frac{8}{6} = 1\frac{2}{6}$ or $1\frac{1}{3}$ laps)

Name _____ Date _____

Multiplying with Fractions

You can use the meaning of multiplication to help you find a fraction of a number.

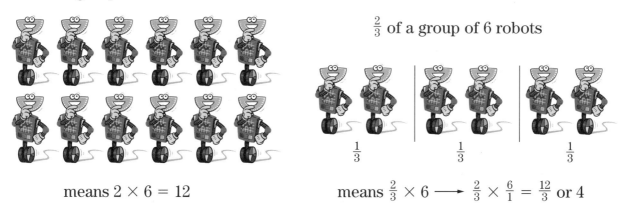

2 groups of 6 robots

$\frac{2}{3}$ of a group of 6 robots

$\frac{1}{3}$ $\frac{1}{3}$ $\frac{1}{3}$

means $2 \times 6 = 12$

means $\frac{2}{3} \times 6 \longrightarrow \frac{2}{3} \times \frac{6}{1} = \frac{12}{3}$ or 4

168 Find the fraction of each number. Write your answer in simplest form.

1. $\frac{1}{3}$ of 9 = ____   2. $\frac{1}{5}$ of 35 = ____   3. $\frac{1}{10}$ of 120 = ____   4. $\frac{1}{4}$ of 16 = ____

5. $\frac{3}{4}$ of 16 = ____   6. $\frac{2}{5}$ of 25 = ____   7. $\frac{2}{3}$ of 96 = ____   8. $\frac{5}{6}$ of 54 = ____

9. $\frac{5}{7}$ of 77 = ____   10. $\frac{5}{6}$ of 72 = ____   11. $\frac{3}{8}$ of 56 = ____   12. $\frac{5}{9}$ of 63 = ____

13. $\frac{2}{3}$ of 40 = ____   14. $\frac{5}{8}$ of 50 = ____   15. $\frac{3}{4}$ of 25 = ____   16. $\frac{2}{5}$ of 28 = ____

17. $\frac{7}{10}$ of 55 = ____   18. $\frac{5}{12}$ of 30 = ____   19. $\frac{7}{16}$ of 44 = ____   20. $\frac{5}{6}$ of 21 = ____

A CD player is advertised for $\frac{1}{4}$ off its regular price of $48.

21. What is the amount of the discount?_____

22. What is the sale price? _____

23. Find $\frac{3}{4}$ of $48. _____

24. Explain why this is the same as $\frac{1}{4}$ off $48. _____

_____

_____

Name _____ Date _____

You can use a picture
to show $\frac{2}{3}$ of $\frac{3}{4}$.

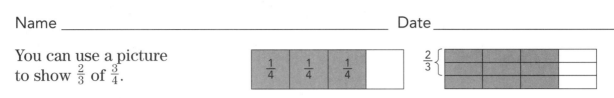

You can also find the answer without
using a picture.

Write the problem as a product.	Multiply numerators. Multiply denominators.	Simplify if possible.
$\frac{2}{3}$ of $\frac{3}{4} \longrightarrow \frac{2}{3} \times \frac{3}{4}$	$\frac{2}{3} \times \frac{3}{4} = \frac{6}{12}$	$\frac{6}{12} \longrightarrow \frac{6 \div 6}{12 \div 6} = \frac{1}{2}$

You can multiply mixed numbers in a similar way.

Multiply: $1\frac{1}{2} \times 2\frac{1}{3}$

Rewrite each mixed number as a fraction.	Multiply numerators. Multiply denominators.	Simplify if possible.
$1\frac{1}{2} \times 2\frac{1}{3} \longrightarrow \frac{3}{2} \times \frac{7}{3}$	$\frac{3}{2} \times \frac{7}{3} = \frac{21}{6}$	$\frac{21}{6} = \frac{21 \div 3}{6 \div 3} = \frac{7}{2}$ or $3\frac{1}{2}$

Multiply. Write your answers in simplest form.

25. $\frac{1}{3} \times \frac{5}{8} =$ _____

26. $\frac{3}{4} \times \frac{1}{5} =$ _____

27. $\frac{3}{10} \times \frac{2}{5} =$ _____

28. $\frac{5}{6} \times \frac{2}{3} =$ _____

29. $\frac{7}{10} \times \frac{1}{2} =$ _____

30. $\frac{5}{12} \times \frac{2}{5} =$ _____

31. $\frac{1}{5} \times 1\frac{1}{2} =$ _____

32. $\frac{1}{8} \times 2\frac{1}{4} =$ _____

33. $\frac{1}{3} \times 3\frac{1}{4} =$ _____

34. $\frac{2}{3} \times 1\frac{5}{8} =$ _____

35. $\frac{3}{4} \times 2\frac{2}{3} =$ _____

36. $\frac{5}{8} \times 2\frac{1}{2} =$ _____

37. $3\frac{1}{3} \times 2 =$ _____

38. $1\frac{3}{4} \times 1\frac{1}{7} =$ _____

39. $2\frac{2}{5} \times 1\frac{1}{8} =$ _____

40. $1\frac{5}{6} \times 2\frac{2}{11} =$ _____

41. $2\frac{3}{4} \times 1\frac{3}{5} =$ _____

42. $3\frac{3}{8} \times 2\frac{2}{3} =$ _____

When adding mixed numbers, you can add the sum of the whole
number parts to the sum of the fraction parts to get the answer.
See if this same procedure works when multiplying mixed numbers
by solving these two problems.

43. $2\frac{1}{2} \times 2\frac{1}{2} =$ _____

44. $(2 \times 2) + (\frac{1}{2} \times \frac{1}{2}) =$ _____

45. When multiplying mixed numbers, can you get the answer by adding the
product of the whole number parts to the product of the fraction parts? _____

169

170

Name _____ Date _____

Multiplying with Fractions

Directions: Solve each problem. Mark your answer.

1 CDs that usually sell for $14 each are on sale at $\frac{1}{2}$ price. What is the sale price of a CD?

- (A) $6
- (B) $7
- (C) $8
- (D) $10

2 Martin ran once around a track that is $\frac{3}{4}$ of a mile long. His little brother Pete ran $\frac{1}{2}$ of the track. How far did Pete run?

- (F) $1\frac{1}{4}$ mi
- (G) $\frac{3}{6}$ mi
- (H) $\frac{1}{3}$ mi
- (I) $\frac{3}{8}$ mi

3 Of the 24 students in Rory's class, $\frac{2}{3}$ are girls. How many girls are in the class?

- (A) 12
- (B) 15
- (C) 16
- (D) 18

4 Stella bought $\frac{3}{8}$ of a pound of grapes and ate $\frac{1}{3}$ of the grapes. How much did she eat?

- (F) $\frac{4}{11}$ lb
- (G) $\frac{3}{11}$ lb
- (H) $\frac{1}{6}$ lb
- (I) $\frac{1}{8}$ lb

5 A nature trail is $1\frac{1}{2}$ miles long. Penny hiked $\frac{3}{5}$ of the trail. How far did she hike?

- (A) $\frac{9}{10}$ mi
- (B) $\frac{3}{5}$ mi
- (C) $\frac{7}{10}$ mi
- (D) $\frac{2}{5}$ mi

6 A hen weighs $2\frac{1}{4}$ pounds. A baby chick weighs $\frac{1}{6}$ as much as the hen. How much does the baby chick weigh?

- (F) $\frac{1}{3}$ lb
- (G) $\frac{3}{8}$ lb
- (H) $\frac{1}{4}$ lb
- (I) $\frac{9}{10}$ lb

PRACTICE ANSWERS
Page 70

1. 3
2. 7
3. 12
4. 4
5. 12
6. 10
7. 64
8. 45
9. 55
10. 60
11. 21
12. 35
13. $26\frac{2}{3}$
14. $31\frac{1}{4}$
15. $18\frac{3}{4}$
16. $11\frac{1}{5}$
17. $38\frac{1}{2}$
18. $12\frac{1}{2}$
19. $19\frac{1}{4}$
20. $17\frac{1}{2}$
21. $12
22. $36
23. $36
24. $\frac{1}{4}$ off means that you are saving $\frac{1}{4}$ of the original price. You are only paying $\frac{3}{4}$ of the original price.

Page 71

25. $\frac{5}{24}$
26. $\frac{3}{20}$
27. $\frac{3}{25}$
28. $\frac{5}{9}$
29. $\frac{7}{20}$
30. $\frac{1}{6}$
31. $\frac{3}{10}$
32. $\frac{9}{32}$
33. $1\frac{1}{12}$
34. $1\frac{1}{12}$
35. 2
36. $1\frac{9}{16}$
37. $6\frac{2}{3}$
38. 2
39. $2\frac{7}{10}$
40. 4
41. $4\frac{2}{5}$
42. 9
43. $6\frac{1}{4}$
44. $4\frac{1}{4}$
45. No

TEST PREP ANSWERS
Page 72

1. B
2. I
3. C
4. I
5. A
6. G

Name _____ Date _____

Dividing with Fractions

Pictures can help you understand how to divide fractions and whole numbers.

Divide: $3 \div \frac{3}{4}$

ONE WAY You can use a picture to find how many $\frac{3}{4}$s are in 3.

$$\frac{3}{4} \quad \frac{3}{4} \quad \frac{3}{4} \quad \frac{3}{4}$$

ANOTHER WAY You can also divide without using a picture. Use the reciprocal of the divisor.

The reciprocal of $\frac{3}{4}$ is $\frac{4}{3}$.

$3 \div \frac{3}{4} \longrightarrow \frac{3}{1} \times \frac{4}{3} = \frac{12}{3}$, or 4.

Divide: $\frac{3}{4} \div 4$

ONE WAY You can use a picture to divide $\frac{3}{4}$ into 4 equal parts.

| $\frac{1}{4}$ | $\frac{1}{4}$ | $\frac{1}{4}$ | |

$\frac{1}{4}$

ANOTHER WAY You can also divide without using a picture. Use the reciprocal of the divisor.

The reciprocal of 4 is $\frac{1}{4}$.

$\frac{3}{4} \div 4 \longrightarrow \frac{3}{4} \times \frac{1}{4} = \frac{3}{16}$.

---

172 Write the reciprocal of each number.

1. $\frac{1}{2}$ Reciprocal = _____ **2.** 7 Reciprocal = _____ **3.** $3\frac{1}{3}$ Reciprocal = _____

173 Rewrite each division problem as the product of two fractions. Then write the answer in simplest form.

4. $5 \div \frac{1}{3} \longrightarrow$ ____ × ____ = ____   **5.** $6 \div \frac{1}{2} \longrightarrow$ ____ × ____ = ____

6. $4 \div \frac{3}{4} \longrightarrow$ ____ × ____ = ____   **7.** $3 \div \frac{3}{8} \longrightarrow$ ____ × ____ = ____

8. $1 \div \frac{5}{6} \longrightarrow$ ____ × ____ = ____   **9.** $2 \div \frac{4}{5} \longrightarrow$ ____ × ____ = ____

174 **10.** $\frac{2}{3} \div 3 \longrightarrow$ ____ × ____ = ____   **11.** $\frac{7}{8} \div 2 \longrightarrow$ ____ × ____ = ____

12. $\frac{3}{5} \div 4 \longrightarrow$ ____ × ____ = ____   **13.** $\frac{9}{10} \div 5 \longrightarrow$ ____ × ____ = ____

14. $\frac{1}{4} \div 10 \longrightarrow$ ____ × ____ = ____   **15.** $\frac{5}{6} \div 8 \longrightarrow$ ____ × ____ = ____

Name _____ Date _____

You can divide fractions and mixed numbers using reciprocals.

Divide: $\frac{2}{3} \div \frac{1}{6}$

Rewrite as a product using the reciprocal of the divisor.	Multiply as usual.	Write in simplest form.
$\frac{2}{3} \div \frac{1}{6} \longrightarrow \frac{2}{3} \times \frac{6}{1}$	$\frac{2}{3} \times \frac{6}{1} = \frac{12}{3}$	$\frac{12}{3} = \frac{4}{1}$, or 4.

Divide: $2\frac{1}{2} \div 1\frac{1}{2}$

Rewrite the mixed numbers as fractions.	Rewrite as a product using the reciprocal of the divisor.	Multiply and simplify.
$2\frac{1}{2} \div 1\frac{1}{2} \longrightarrow \frac{5}{2} \div \frac{3}{2}$	$\frac{5}{2} \div \frac{3}{2} \longrightarrow \frac{5}{2} \times \frac{2}{3}$	$\frac{5}{2} \times \frac{2}{3} = \frac{10}{6} = \frac{5}{3}$, or $1\frac{2}{3}$

Rewrite each division problem as a product.
Then write the answer in simplest form.

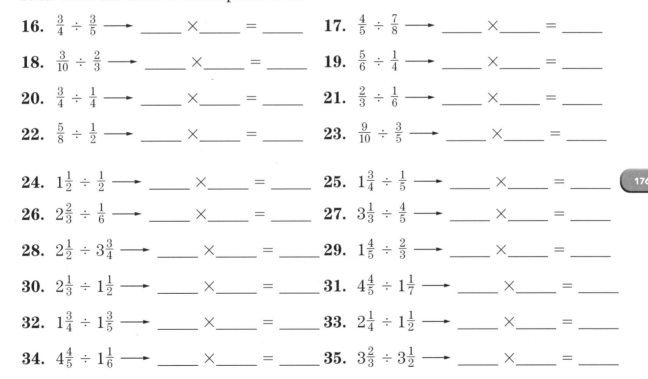

16. $\frac{3}{4} \div \frac{3}{5} \longrightarrow$ _____ × _____ = _____   17. $\frac{4}{5} \div \frac{7}{8} \longrightarrow$ _____ × _____ = _____

18. $\frac{3}{10} \div \frac{2}{3} \longrightarrow$ _____ × _____ = _____   19. $\frac{5}{6} \div \frac{1}{4} \longrightarrow$ _____ × _____ = _____

20. $\frac{3}{4} \div \frac{1}{4} \longrightarrow$ _____ × _____ = _____   21. $\frac{2}{3} \div \frac{1}{6} \longrightarrow$ _____ × _____ = _____

22. $\frac{5}{8} \div \frac{1}{2} \longrightarrow$ _____ × _____ = _____   23. $\frac{9}{10} \div \frac{3}{5} \longrightarrow$ _____ × _____ = _____

24. $1\frac{1}{2} \div \frac{1}{2} \longrightarrow$ _____ × _____ = _____   25. $1\frac{3}{4} \div \frac{1}{5} \longrightarrow$ _____ × _____ = _____

26. $2\frac{2}{3} \div \frac{1}{6} \longrightarrow$ _____ × _____ = _____   27. $3\frac{1}{3} \div \frac{4}{5} \longrightarrow$ _____ × _____ = _____

28. $2\frac{1}{2} \div 3\frac{3}{4} \longrightarrow$ _____ × _____ = _____   29. $1\frac{4}{5} \div \frac{2}{3} \longrightarrow$ _____ × _____ = _____

30. $2\frac{1}{3} \div 1\frac{1}{2} \longrightarrow$ _____ × _____ = _____   31. $4\frac{4}{5} \div 1\frac{1}{7} \longrightarrow$ _____ × _____ = _____

32. $1\frac{3}{4} \div 1\frac{3}{5} \longrightarrow$ _____ × _____ = _____   33. $2\frac{1}{4} \div 1\frac{1}{2} \longrightarrow$ _____ × _____ = _____

34. $4\frac{4}{5} \div 1\frac{1}{6} \longrightarrow$ _____ × _____ = _____   35. $3\frac{2}{3} \div 3\frac{1}{2} \longrightarrow$ _____ × _____ = _____

36. Take a look at the problems and solutions for questions 16−35. Write a brief explanation of how you can tell if a division problem will have a quotient greater than 1.

_____

_____

175

176

Name _____ Date _____

Dividing with Fractions

Directions: Solve each problem. Write your answer.

1. Jan made 4 cups of banana pudding. How many $\frac{1}{2}$-cup servings can she serve?

   _____

2. Pierre has 3 ounces of chili powder for cooking. He wants to store it in bags with $\frac{1}{4}$ ounce in each bag. How many bags will he need?

   _____

3. Suki made 5 pounds of potato salad. If she puts $\frac{2}{3}$ of a pound of potato salad in each container, how many containers will she fill?

   _____

4. A dump truck delivers $\frac{3}{4}$ of a ton of sand. If the sand is divided into 6 equal piles, how much will each pile weigh?

   _____

5. Mrs. Lopez bought $\frac{1}{2}$ pound of shrimp. If she puts $\frac{1}{8}$ pound of shrimp on each plate, how many plates can she fill?

   _____

6. Mr. Meyers made $\frac{3}{5}$ of a gallon of grape juice. He wants to pour it into bottles that hold $\frac{1}{10}$ gallon each. How many bottles can he fill?

   _____

7. A race track is $1\frac{1}{4}$ miles long. There is a red post marking every $\frac{1}{16}$ of a mile. How many red posts are there in all?

   _____

8. A wall made of cinder blocks is 15 feet long. Each block is $1\frac{1}{2}$ feet long. How many blocks are needed to make a 15-foot row?

   _____

PRACTICE ANSWERS
Page 74

1. $\frac{2}{1}$

2. $\frac{1}{7}$

3. $\frac{3}{10}$

4. $\frac{5}{1} \times \frac{3}{1} = 15$

5. $\frac{6}{1} \times \frac{2}{1} = 12$

6. $\frac{4}{1} \times \frac{4}{3} = 5\frac{1}{3}$

7. $\frac{3}{1} \times \frac{8}{3} = 8$

8. $\frac{1}{1} \times \frac{6}{5} = 1\frac{1}{5}$

9. $\frac{2}{1} \times \frac{5}{4} = 2\frac{1}{2}$

10. $\frac{2}{3} \times \frac{1}{3} = \frac{2}{9}$

11. $\frac{7}{8} \times \frac{1}{2} = \frac{7}{16}$

12. $\frac{3}{5} \times \frac{1}{4} = \frac{3}{20}$

13. $\frac{9}{10} \times \frac{1}{5} = \frac{9}{50}$

14. $\frac{1}{4} \times \frac{1}{10} = \frac{1}{40}$

15. $\frac{5}{6} \times \frac{1}{8} = \frac{5}{48}$

Page 75

16. $\frac{3}{4} \times \frac{5}{3} = 1\frac{1}{4}$

17. $\frac{4}{5} \times \frac{8}{7} = \frac{32}{35}$

18. $\frac{3}{10} \times \frac{3}{2} = \frac{9}{20}$

19. $\frac{5}{6} \times \frac{4}{1} = 3\frac{1}{3}$

20. $\frac{3}{4} \times \frac{4}{1} = 3$

21. $\frac{2}{3} \times \frac{6}{1} = 4$

22. $\frac{5}{8} \times \frac{2}{1} = 1\frac{1}{4}$

23. $\frac{9}{10} \times \frac{5}{3} = 1\frac{1}{2}$

24. $\frac{3}{2} \times \frac{2}{1} = 3$

25. $\frac{7}{4} \times \frac{5}{1} = 8\frac{3}{4}$

26. $\frac{8}{3} \times \frac{6}{1} = 16$

27. $\frac{10}{3} \times \frac{5}{4} = 4\frac{1}{6}$

28. $\frac{5}{2} \times \frac{4}{15} = \frac{2}{3}$

29. $\frac{9}{5} \times \frac{3}{2} = 2\frac{7}{10}$

30. $\frac{7}{3} \times \frac{2}{3} = 1\frac{5}{9}$

31. $\frac{24}{5} \times \frac{7}{8} = 4\frac{1}{5}$

32. $\frac{7}{4} \times \frac{5}{8} = 1\frac{3}{32}$

33. $\frac{9}{4} \times \frac{2}{3} = 1\frac{1}{2}$

34. $\frac{24}{5} \times \frac{6}{7} = 4\frac{4}{35}$

35. $\frac{11}{3} \times \frac{2}{7} = 1\frac{1}{21}$

36. When the divisor is less than the dividend, the quotient will be greater than 1.

TEST PREP ANSWERS
Page 76

1. 8 servings

2. 12 bags

3. $7\frac{1}{2}$ containers

4. $\frac{1}{8}$ ton

5. 4 plates

6. 6 bottles

7. 20 red posts

8. 10 blocks

Sliding Rulers

OBJECTIVES
- Add and subtract fractions
- See that addition and subtraction are opposite operations

MATERIALS
- two rulers for each student

TIME
- 45–60 minutes

TEACHER NOTES
- In this activity, students use a concrete manipulative to help them see how to add and subtract fractions.

- Because the relative size of each fractional part is the same on the rulers, students will not be confused by the distortion that can result when they try to use fractions circles they have drawn to solve problems.

- This is a good opportunity to review perimeter.

EXTENSIONS
- See if the students can find a way to use the rulers to facilitate multiplication of fractions.

- Demonstrate a division problem using the rulers. Ask the students to tell if the dividend is greater than or less than the quotient. Ask them to explain what they notice.

- Have the students pretend that one of their rulers is broken and begins at the $2\frac{1}{4}$ in. mark. Have them use this broken ruler as one of the two rulers used to add and subtract fractions.

- Demonstrate the use of a slide rule. Compare its use with the sliding rulers used in this activity.

- Have the students calculate the inside perimeter of the picture frame Cindy's mother is covering if the frame is one inch wide on all sides.

ANSWERS

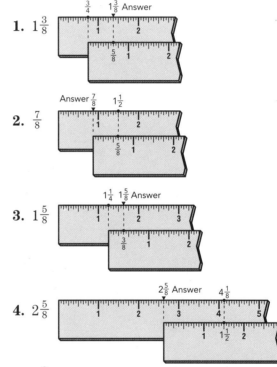

1. $1\frac{3}{8}$

2. $\frac{7}{8}$

3. $1\frac{5}{8}$

4. $2\frac{5}{8}$

5. $1\frac{3}{4}$

6. Since addition and subtraction are inverse operations, the rulers will look the same if adding $1\frac{3}{4}$ and $3\frac{3}{4}$ or subtracting $3\frac{3}{4}$ from $5\frac{1}{2}$. (Students may think that the rulers show the subtraction problem $9\frac{1}{4}$ minus $3\frac{3}{4}$, but the fraction on the bottom ruler when subtracting needs to be the larger of the two numbers.)

7. $26\frac{3}{4}$ in. If possible, demonstrate this addition by using two yardsticks and following the procedure outlined here.

Name _____ Date _____

Sliding Rulers

Fractions: 028

Fractions on a Number
Line: 031

Fractions Greater than
One: 034

Least Common
Denominator: 036

Adding with Fractions:
157–161

Subtracting with
Fractions: 162–166

Cindy watched as her mother figured out how much ribbon it would take to cover the perimeter of a $5\frac{1}{8}$ in. by $8\frac{1}{4}$ in. picture frame. Instead of computing the perimeter, Cindy's mother measured the length of one side directly on the yardstick, held her place, slid the yardstick to measure the next side, and so on. Cindy realized that she could add fractions in a similar way by using two rulers. Here's how she used the rulers to add $1\frac{1}{2}$ and $\frac{3}{4}$.

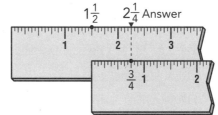

Cindy soon discovered that she could use the rulers to subtract fractions as well. Here's how she subtracted $1\frac{3}{4}$ from $3\frac{3}{8}$.

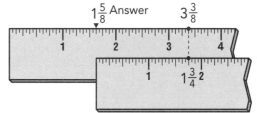

Addition Steps

A. Identify one of the fractions on each ruler.

B. Line up the zero end of the top ruler with the mark for the first fraction on the bottom ruler.

C. Find the mark for the second fraction on the top ruler.

D. Let your eye connect the mark on the top ruler with the one directly above it on the bottom ruler to get the sum.

Subtraction Steps

A. Identify the larger fraction on the bottom ruler. Find the mark for the second fraction on the top ruler.

B. Line up the marks for the fractions on both rulers.

C. Look at the zero end of the top ruler.

D. Let your eye connect the zero end of the top ruler with the mark directly above it on the bottom ruler to get the difference.

Use Cindy's system to solve these problems.

1. $\frac{3}{4} + \frac{5}{8}$ _____

2. $1\frac{1}{2} - \frac{5}{8}$ _____

3. $1\frac{1}{4} + \frac{3}{8}$ _____

4. $4\frac{1}{8} - 1\frac{1}{2}$ _____

5. Suppose that two rulers are lined up with the $5\frac{1}{2}$ mark on the bottom ruler and the $3\frac{3}{4}$ mark on the top ruler. What is the missing fraction? _____

6. Can you tell from how the rulers are arranged if the fractions are being added or subtracted?

   Explain why you think so. _____

   _____

7. By the way, how much ribbon did Cindy's mother need to cover the perimeter of the picture frame? _____

Name _____ Date _____

Ratio

Brad and Sue like to collect coins, stamps, and sports cards. They can compare their collections using ratios. They can write each ratio 3 ways.

Number of Items Collected				
	Coins	Stamps	Sports Cards	Total
Brad	150	25	5	180
Sue	100	25	15	140

Brad's coins to Sue's coins:	**Brad's stamps to his whole collection:**	**Brad's total to Sue's total:**
150 to 100	25 to 180	180 to 140
150:100	25:180	180:140
$\frac{150}{100}$	$\frac{25}{180}$	$\frac{180}{140}$
This is a part-to-part ratio.	This is a part-to-whole ratio.	This is a whole-to-whole ratio.

178-179 Use the table above. Write a ratio for each comparison in 3 ways.
Tell whether it is a part-to-part, a part-to-whole, or a whole-to-whole ratio.

Brad's stamps to Sue's stamps:

   1. Ratio _____   **2.** Type _____

Sue's total to Brad's total:

   3. Ratio _____   **4.** Type _____

Sue's stamps to her total collection:

   5. Ratio _____   **6.** Type _____

When comparing amounts that use different units of measure, you need to include the units in the ratio. This is called a rate. For example, to compare the amount of baking mix to the number of eggs, write

   3 cups to 2 eggs, or 3 cups:2 eggs, or $\frac{3 \text{ cups}}{2 \text{ eggs}}$

BEST EVER MUFFINS
3 cups baking mix
1 cup milk
2 eggs
3 tablespoons cooking oil
5 tablespoons sugar

180 Write a ratio to compare the amounts.
Write each ratio three ways.

   7. Baking mix to milk _____

   8. Eggs to milk _____

   9. Milk to oil _____

Name _____ Date _____

Ratio

Directions: The chart below shows how many kinds of stuffed animals Lola and her friend Julie have. Use the chart to answer the questions.

Stuffed Animals	Lola	Julie
Bears	6	4
Birds	2	3
Dogs	5	3
Cats	3	5
Frogs	4	0
Totals	20	15

1. In Lola's collection, what is the ratio of dogs to all animals?

    A   5:15

    B   1:3

    C   6:20

    D   1:4

2. What is the ratio of Lola's bears to her frogs?

    E   3:2

    F   6:5

    G   4:1

    H   1:5

3. What is the ratio of animals in Lola's collection to animals in Julie's collection?

    A   5:3

    B   4:3

    C   3:5

    D   3:4

4. In Julie's collection, what is the ratio of cats to all animals?

    E $\frac{1}{4}$

    F $\frac{1}{5}$

    G $\frac{1}{3}$

    H $\frac{1}{6}$

5. Find the ratio of Julie's birds to all of her animals.

    A $\frac{1}{5}$

    B $\frac{3}{1}$

    C $\frac{1}{4}$

    D $\frac{5}{1}$

6. What is the ratio of Lola's cats to Julie's cats?

    E   2 to 3

    F   1 to 2

    G   3 to 5

    H   5 to 3

PRACTICE ANSWERS
Page 80

1. 25 to 25 or 1 to 1; 25:25 or 1:1; $\frac{25}{25}$ or $\frac{1}{1}$

2. Part-to-part

3. 140 to 180 or 7 to 9; 140:180 or 7:9; $\frac{140}{180}$ or $\frac{7}{9}$

4. Whole-to-whole

5. 25 to 140 or 5 to 28; 25:140 or 5:28; $\frac{25}{140}$ or $\frac{5}{28}$

6. Part-to-whole

7. 3 to 1; 3:1; $\frac{3}{1}$

8. 2 eggs to 1 cup; 2 eggs:1 cup; $\frac{2 \text{ eggs}}{1 \text{ cup}}$

9. 1 cup to 3 tablespoons; 1 cup:3 tablespoons; $\frac{1 \text{ cup}}{3 \text{ tablespoons}}$

TEST PREP ANSWERS
Page 81

1. D

2. E

3. B

4. G

5. A

6. G

Name _____ Date _____

Proportion

You can solve proportions in two ways.

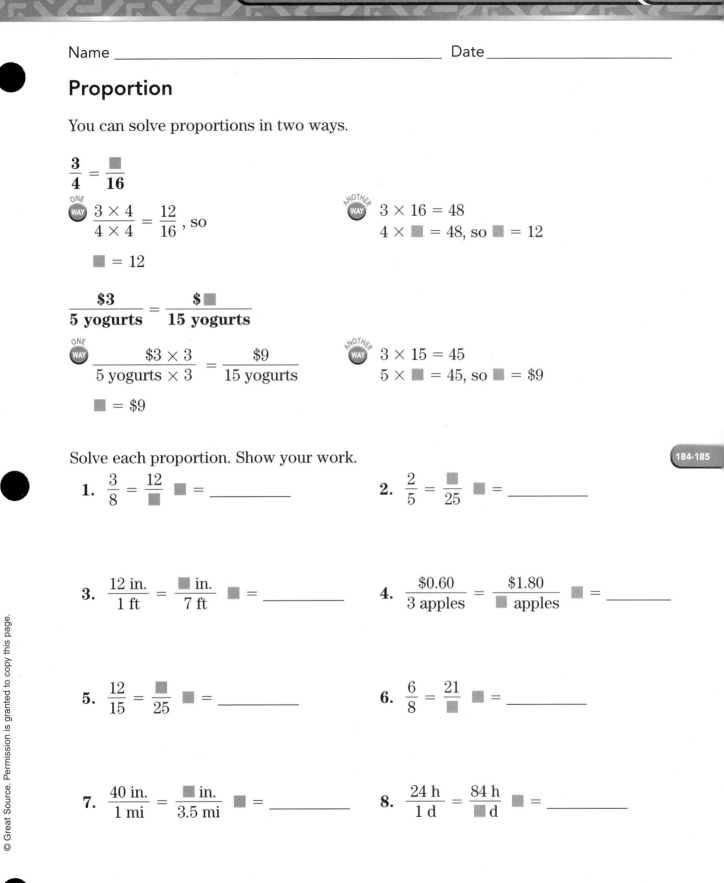

$$\frac{3}{4} = \frac{\blacksquare}{16}$$

ONE WAY $\frac{3 \times 4}{4 \times 4} = \frac{12}{16}$, so

$\blacksquare = 12$

ANOTHER WAY $3 \times 16 = 48$

$4 \times \blacksquare = 48$, so $\blacksquare = 12$

$$\frac{\$3}{5 \text{ yogurts}} = \frac{\$\blacksquare}{15 \text{ yogurts}}$$

ONE WAY $\frac{\$3 \times 3}{5 \text{ yogurts} \times 3} = \frac{\$9}{15 \text{ yogurts}}$

$\blacksquare = \$9$

ANOTHER WAY $3 \times 15 = 45$

$5 \times \blacksquare = 45$, so $\blacksquare = \$9$

Solve each proportion. Show your work.

184-185

1. $\frac{3}{8} = \frac{12}{\blacksquare}$ $\blacksquare = $ _____

2. $\frac{2}{5} = \frac{\blacksquare}{25}$ $\blacksquare = $ _____

3. $\frac{12 \text{ in.}}{1 \text{ ft}} = \frac{\blacksquare \text{ in.}}{7 \text{ ft}}$ $\blacksquare = $ _____

4. $\frac{\$0.60}{3 \text{ apples}} = \frac{\$1.80}{\blacksquare \text{ apples}}$ $\blacksquare = $ _____

5. $\frac{12}{15} = \frac{\blacksquare}{25}$ $\blacksquare = $ _____

6. $\frac{6}{8} = \frac{21}{\blacksquare}$ $\blacksquare = $ _____

7. $\frac{40 \text{ in.}}{1 \text{ mi}} = \frac{\blacksquare \text{ in.}}{3.5 \text{ mi}}$ $\blacksquare = $ _____

8. $\frac{24 \text{ h}}{1 \text{ d}} = \frac{84 \text{ h}}{\blacksquare \text{ d}}$ $\blacksquare = $ _____

Name _____ Date _____

A box of cereal costs $3.60 for 16 oz. What is the unit price of the cereal?

price ⟶ **$3.60** = **$■** ⟵ price
weight ⟶ **16 oz**   **1 oz** ⟵ weight

ONE WAY 1 × $3.60 = $3.60
16 × ■ = $3.60
Divide $3.60 by 16 to find ■.
The unit price is $0.225

ANOTHER WAY Since 16 oz cost $3.60, divide by 16 to find the cost of 1 oz (the unit price).
$3.60 ÷ 16 = $0.225

An "O" gauge model train uses a scale of 10 ft = 1 in.
One model engine is 7 inches long. How long is the real engine?

scale length ⟶ **1 in.** = **7 in.** ⟵ scale length
real length ⟶ **10 ft**   **■ ft** ⟵ real length

ONE WAY $\frac{1 \text{ in.} \times 7}{10 \text{ ft} \times 7} = \frac{7 \text{ in.}}{70 \text{ ft}}$
So the real engine is 70 ft long.

ANOTHER WAY 10 × 7 = 70
1 × ■ = 70, so ■ = 70 ft, the length of the real engine.

186 Find the unit price of each package. Show the proportion you used.

9. 6 pastries cost $0.99

10. 8 oz of salad dressing cost $1.20

_____

_____

11. 6 oz of cocoa cost $2.25

12. 8 dinner rolls cost $0.84

_____

_____

13. 4.5 oz of cheese cost $1.89

14. 50 oz of dishwasher soap cost $2.68

_____

_____

187 A map has a scale of 1 in. = 20 mi. Find each distance.

15. Map distance is 6 in.
Real distance is _____

16. Real distance is 15 mi.
Map distance is _____

17. Map distance is $3\frac{1}{2}$ in.
Real distance is _____

18. Real distance is 36 mi.
Map distance is _____

Name _____ Date _____

Proportion

Directions: Solve each problem. Use pictures, words, or numbers to show your answer.

1. Terry has a rectangular garden that measures 24 ft × 10 ft. She wants to make it twice as large but keep it the same shape. What will be the dimensions of her new garden?

2. Charles is making pancakes. He needs 1 egg for every 5 pancakes. How many eggs will he need for 20 pancakes?

3. Ted makes 5 quarts of orange paint by mixing 3 quarts of red and 2 quarts of yellow. How many quarts of each color paint will he need to make 25 quarts of orange paint?

4. Mickey's dad was driving a truck at 45 miles per hour. At that rate, how far would he travel in 6 hours?

5. Find the unit price for each box of cereal.

6. Nancy is making a scale drawing of a rectangular deck that is 16 ft wide and 20 ft long. At a scale of 1 inch = 4 feet, what will be the width and length of her scale drawing?

PRACTICE ANSWERS
Page 83

1. ■ = 32
2. ■ = 10
3. ■ = 84 in.
4. ■ = 9 apples
5. ■ = 20
6. ■ = 28
7. ■ = 140 in.
8. ■ = $3\frac{1}{2}$ days

Page 84

9. ■ = $0.165
10. ■ = $0.15
11. ■ = $0.375
12. ■ = $0.105
13. ■ = $0.42
14. ■ = $0.0536
15. 120 mi
16. $\frac{3}{4}$ in.
17. 70 mi
18. $1\frac{4}{5}$ in.

TEST PREP ANSWERS
Page 85

1. 48 ft × 20 ft
2. 4 eggs
3. 15 qt red paint and 10 qt yellow paint
4. 270 miles
5. Granola = $0.15/oz; Wheat Flakes = $0.23/oz
6. 4 in. × 5 in.

Name _____ Date _____

Percent

36% means 36 parts out of 100.
You can write 36% as the ratio $\frac{36}{100}$.

Find 36% of 50 pens. First write a proportion.
Use the percent ratio.

36% is shaded.

part ⟶ $\frac{\mathbf{36}}{\mathbf{100}}$ = $\frac{\blacksquare}{\mathbf{50}}$ ⟵ part
whole ⟶ ⟵ whole

ONE WAY $\frac{36 \div 2}{100 \div 2} = \frac{18}{50}$

So, 36% of 50 pens is 18 pens.

ANOTHER WAY $36 \times 50 = 1800$
$100 \times \blacksquare = 1800$
So, $\blacksquare = 18$ pens.

Shade each percent.

190

1. 24%   **2.** 40%   **3.** 35%

Find the percent of each number. Show the proportion you use.

193

4. 15% of 80 _____   **5.** 90% of 120 _____   **6.** 60% of 45 _____

7. 12% of 44 _____   **8.** 38% of 105 _____   **9.** 55% of 92 _____

10. 5% of 160 _____   **11.** 8% of 95 _____   **12.** 3% of 25 _____

13. 125% of 64 _____   **14.** 240% of 35 _____   **15.** 112% of 204 _____

16. 12.5% of 60 _____ **17.** 1.5% of 90 _____   **18.** 0.5% of 75 _____

Name _____   Date _____

18 is what percent of 24?

The number line at the right can help you see the answer. Or you can use these steps.

25%	25%	25%	25%

0   6   12   18   24

Write the percent as a ratio.

$$\frac{\blacksquare}{100}$$

Write the proportion.

$$\frac{\blacksquare}{100} = \frac{18}{24}$$

Solve the proportion.

$100 \times 18 = 1800$

$\blacksquare \times 24 = 1800$

$\blacksquare = 1800 \div 24$, or 75

So, 18 is 75% of 24.

22 is 40% of what number?

You need to find the whole. The number lines at the right can help you see the answer. Or you can use these steps.

20%	20%

0   11   22

20%	20%	20%	20%

0   11   22   33   44

Write the percent as a ratio.

$$\frac{40}{100}$$

Write the proportion.

$$\frac{40}{100} = \frac{22}{\blacksquare}$$

Solve the proportion.

$100 \times 22 = 2200$

$40 \times \blacksquare = 2200$

$\blacksquare = 2200 \div 40$, or 55

So, 22 is 40% of 55.

194-195   Find the percent or the whole. Show the proportion you use.

19. 13 is what percent of 65? _____   **20.** 15 is 30% of what number? _____

21. 24 is 12% of what number? _____   **22.** 36 is what percent of 96? _____

23. 42 is what percent of 280? _____   **24.** 49 is what percent of 175? _____

25. 180 is 144% of what number? _____   **26.** 39 is 260% of what number? _____

Name _____   Date _____

**Find the amount of simple interest on a loan
of $500 borrowed for 6 months at 8% interest.**

Use the formula: Interest = principal × rate × time, or $I = p\,r\,t$
(r is the annual interest rate, written in decimal form. t is the time in years.)

$I = p \times r \times t$ You will need to repay $20
$I = 500 \times 0.08 \times \frac{1}{2}$ in interest plus the $500 at the
$I = 20$ end of the 6-month period.

**A CD player originally sold for $80. This week
it is discounted 15%. What does it cost now?**

Calculate the amount of the discount.   Subtract to find the sale price.

15% of $80 = $80 × 0.15   Original price − discount = sale price
       = $12 $80 − $12   = $68

Find the interest on each deposit or loan amount.   196

27. A deposit of $240 at 6% for 2 years   **28.** A loan of $1020 at 9% for 18 months

Interest: _____   Interest: _____

29. A deposit of $3200 at 4% for 5 years   **30.** A loan of $850 at 12% for 3 months

Interest: _____   Interest: _____

Find the sale price of each item.   197

31. Original price: $50   **32.** Original price: $125
Discount: 25%   Discount: 20%
Sale price: _____   Sale price: _____

33. Original price: $45   **34.** Original price: $15
Discount: 15%   Discount: 30%
Sale price: _____   Sale price: _____

35. Original price: $280   **36.** Original price: $78
Discount: 35%   Discount: 10%
Sale price: _____   Sale price: _____

Name _____ Date _____

Percent

Directions: Solve each problem. Mark the letter for your answer.

1 Karen has $80. She wants to spend 40% of that amount on clothes. How much can she spend on clothes?

    A $20

    B $32

    C $36

    D $50

2 What is 25% of 96?

    F 20

    G 23

    H 24

    J 28

3 What is 12% of 50?

    A 6

    B 8

    C 10

    D 12

4 Leon has a collection of 40 CDs. 8 of the CDs are jazz. What percent of Leon's collection is jazz?

    F 5%

    G 20%

    H 25%

    J 32%

5 Of the 30 students in the band, 3 play drums. What percent of the students play drums?

    A 5%

    B 6%

    C 9%

    D 10%

6 In a parking lot, 30 cars are blue. Blue cars make up 40% of the total number of cars. How many cars are in the lot?

    F 40

    G 60

    H 75

    J 100

7 Maxine has $500 in a savings account. It earns 4% simple interest per year. How much will be in her account at the end of a year?

    A $504.00

    B $512.50

    C $520.00

    D $540.00

8 A pair of shoes is on sale at a discount of 25%. If the original price of the shoes was $60, what is the sale price?

    F $15

    G $30

    H $42

    J $45

PRACTICE ANSWERS
Page 87

1.

2.

3.

4. 12
5. 108
6. 27
7. 5.28
8. 39.9
9. 50.6
10. 8
11. 7.6
12. 0.75, or $\frac{3}{4}$
13. 80
14. 84
15. 228.48
16. 7.5
17. 1.35
18. 0.375

Page 88

19. 20%
20. 50
21. 200
22. 37.5%
23. 15%
24. 28%
25. 125
26. 15

Page 89

27. $28.80
28. $137.70
29. $640
30. $25.50
31. $37.50
32. $100
33. $38.25
34. $10.50
35. $182
36. $70.20

TEST PREP ANSWERS
Page 90

1. B
2. H
3. A
4. G
5. D
6. H
7. C
8. J

A Nutritional Kick

OBJECTIVES
- Estimate and compute with percents
- Use unit rate to determine number of calories

MATERIALS
- Math Notebook Page, page 190
- calculators

TIME
- 30–45 minutes

TEACHER NOTES
- The suggestion of 2500 calories as a daily total was made by a dietitian in a pediatric hospital. Other daily totals are possible.

- The 50% carbohydrate, 25% protein, and 25% fat figures have been selected to provide benchmark percents for easy computation and estimation. Nutritionists use a wide variety of suggested percentages depending on the situation involved. For example, athletes often eat a higher amount of carbohydrate during training.

- Additional information can be found on nutrition labels on food products, including the percent of daily value based on a 2000 calorie diet.

EXTENSIONS
- Have the students list the food they eat in a day and determine the nutritional content.

- Using real nutrition labels, have the students create a menu for a day that includes all the nutritional quantities.

- Have the students investigate nutritional information for common foods such as fruits, meat, vegetables, cheese, and milk.

- Have students research the nutritional value of the food at their favorite fast-food restaurant.

- Have the students investigate training diets used by famous athletes.

ANSWERS
1. About 1250 calories. Accept all reasonable estimates.

2. About 625 calories. Accept all reasonable estimates.

3. Fruit bars, Lucky Loops Cereal, cheese macaroni, and butter crackers

4. No. 2 grams of protein in the fruit bar and 12 grams of protein in the cheese macaroni is a total of 14 grams of protein. The total weight of the two servings is 107 grams. Jeffrey needs 27 grams of protein to equal 25% protein.

5. No. He eats 48 grams of food, and 17 grams of carbohydrate. This is only about 25% carbohydrate content.

6. 240 calories

7. The total weight is 185 grams, with 119 grams of carbohydrate. A good estimate is about 60%. The actual (rounded) percent is 64%.

Name _____ Date _____

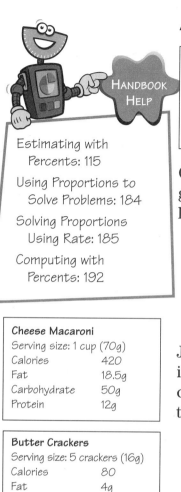

Estimating with
Percents: 115

Using Proportions to
Solve Problems: 184

Solving Proportions
Using Rate: 185

Computing with
Percents: 192

Cheese Macaroni
Serving size: 1 cup (70g)
Calories   420
Fat   18.5g
Carbohydrate   50g
Protein   12g

Butter Crackers
Serving size: 5 crackers (16g)
Calories   80
Fat   4g
Carbohydrate   10g
Protein   1g

Fruit Bars
Serving size: 1 bar (37g)
Calories   140
Fat   3g
Carbohydrate   27g
Protein   2g

Lucky Loops Cereal
Serving size: 1 cup (30g)
Calories   120
Fat   1g
Carbohydrate   25g
Protein   2g

Peanut Butter
Serving size: 2 Tbs. (32g)
Calories   190
Fat   16g
Carbohydrate   7g
Protein   8g

A Nutritional Kick

Suggested Daily Nutritional Values	Suggested Daily Nutritional Values for Athletes in Training	Coach Scott's Daily Plan
65% carbohydrate	40% carbohydrate	2500 calories
15% protein	30% protein	50% carbohydrate
20% fat	30% fat	25% protein
		25% fat

Coach Scott is very concerned that his soccer players practice good nutrition. He showed the players how to read nutrition labels on food packages.

1. About how many calories of carbohydrate does Coach Scott suggest the players eat each day? _____

2. In the coach's plan, about how many calories of protein should be eaten each day? _____

Jeffrey, one of the soccer players, decides to use the nutrition information on the packages of the food he eats to help him choose better meals. Use the sample nutrition labels to the left to answer these questions.

3. Which foods are at least 50% carbohydrate? _____

4. Jeffrey has a fruit bar and a serving of cheese macaroni for lunch. Is the protein content of this meal 25% of the whole meal by weight? _____

On your Math Notebook Page, explain how you got your answer.

5. Jeffrey eats a serving of butter crackers and a serving of peanut butter as an afternoon snack. Is the carbohydrate content of this snack 50% of the whole snack by weight? _____

On your Math Notebook Page, explain how you got your answer.

6. Jeffrey eats two servings of Lucky Loops Cereal for breakfast. How many calories is that? _____

7. Jeffrey eats one serving of each item. Estimate what percent of the total is carbohydrate. Then calculate the actual percent.

   Estimate _____   Actual percent _____

Name _____ Date _____

Integers

Add: ⁻5 + 7

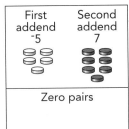

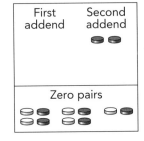

Use 5 negative counters.   Use 7 positive counters.

Form 5 zero pairs. Two positive counters remain. The sum is 2.

Subtract: ⁻6 − (⁻2)

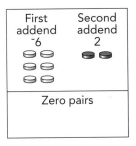

⁻6 − ⁻2 = ⁻6 + 2

First rewrite using addition. Add the opposite of ⁻2.   Use 6 negative counters.   Use 2 positive counters.

Form 2 zero pairs. Four negative counters remain. The difference is ⁻4.

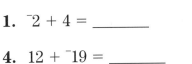 **203-205**   Add.

1. ⁻2 + 4 = _____   **2.** ⁻5 + ⁻3 = _____   **3.** ⁻6 + 4 = _____

4. 12 + ⁻19 = _____   **5.** ⁻25 + 17 = _____   **6.** ⁻23 + ⁻54 = _____

207-209   Rewrite these subtraction problems as addition problems. Then solve.

7. 3 − 4 = ____ + ____ = ____   **8.** ⁻6 − 2 = ____ + ____ = ____

9. 1 − ⁻3 = ____ + ____ = ____   **10.** ⁻5 − ⁻4 = ____ + ____ = ____

11. ⁻3 − 7 = ____ + ____ = ____   **12.** 5 − ⁻2 = ____ + ____ = ____

Name _____ Date _____

Use these rules when multiplying or dividing integers.

• Positive × positive = positive
• Negative × negative = positive
• Positive × negative = negative

• Positive ÷ positive = positive
• Negative ÷ negative = positive
• Negative ÷ positive, or   positive ÷ negative = negative

7 × $^-$5
Since 7 and $^-$5 have different signs, their product is negative.
7 × 5 is 35, so 7 × $^-$5 = $^-$35.

$^-$33 ÷ $^-$11
Since $^-$33 and $^-$11 have the same sign, their quotient is positive.
33 ÷ 11 is 3, so $^-$33 ÷ $^-$11 = 3.

Find each product or quotient.   `210-211`

13. $^-$1 × $^-$1 = _____   **14.** $^-$8 × $^-$6 = _____   **15.** 24 ÷ $^-$3 = _____

16. $^-$96 ÷ 12 = _____   **17.** $^-$85 ÷ $^-$5 = _____   **18.** $^-$12 × $^-$12 = _____

19. 240 ÷ $^-$8 = _____   **20.** $^-$180 ÷ $^-$15 = _____   **21.** $^-$25 × $^-$13 = _____

22. $^-$22 × 9 = _____   **23.** 1008 ÷ 16 = _____   **24.** 17 × 5 = _____

25. 10 × $^-$508 = _____   **26.** $^-$396 ÷ $^-$18 = _____   **27.** $^-$12,320 ÷ 11 = _____

Find each answer. Work from left to right.   `210-211`

$^-$8 × 2 ÷ $^-$1 =
$^-$16 ÷ $^-$1 =
16

28. $^-$2 × $^-$2 × $^-$2 = _____

29. $^-$96 ÷ $^-$24 × $^-$3 = _____   **30.** $^-$9 × $^-$7 × $^-$2 = _____

31. $^-$56 ÷ $^-$7 ÷ $^-$4 = _____   **32.** 150 ÷ $^-$25 × 2 ÷ $^-$4 = _____

33. $^-$8 × 6 ÷ 16 = _____   **34.** 25 × 25 ÷ $^-$5 ÷ $^-$5 = _____

35. $^-$3 × $^-$3 × $^-$3 × $^-$3 = _____   **36.** $^-$18 × 5 ÷ $^-$3 ÷ $^-$10 = _____

Name _____ Date _____

Integers

Directions: Solve each problem. Mark the letter for your answer.
If your answer is not given, mark "None of these."

1 $^-16 + 24 =$
- A $^-8$
- B 8
- C $^-40$
- D 40
- E None of these

2 $52 + {}^-7 =$
- F $^-59$
- G 59
- H 45
- J $^-45$
- K None of these

3 $^-33 + {}^-9 =$
- A $^-42$
- B 42
- C $^-24$
- D 24
- E None of these

4 $^-20 - 8 =$
- F 28
- G $^-12$
- H 12
- J $^-28$
- K None of these

5 $15 - {}^-6 =$
- A $^-21$
- B 11
- C $^-9$
- D 9
- E None of these

6 $^-38 + {}^-17 =$
- F $^-15$
- G 15
- H $^-55$
- J 55
- K None of these

7 $^-4 \times 9 =$
- A 5
- B $^-13$
- C $^-5$
- D 36
- E None of these

8 $^-10 \times {}^-25 =$
- F $^-15$
- G 15
- H $^-250$
- J 250
- K None of these

9 $^-32 \div 8 =$
- A 4
- B $^-4$
- C 256
- D $^-256$
- E None of these

10 $^-40 \div {}^-5 =$
- F 200
- G $^-200$
- H 8
- J $^-8$
- K None of these

PRACTICE ANSWERS
Page 94

1. 2
2. ⁻8
3. ⁻2
4. ⁻7
5. ⁻8
6. ⁻77
7. 3 + ⁻4 = ⁻1
8. ⁻6 + ⁻2 = ⁻8
9. 1 + 3 = 4
10. ⁻5 + 4 = ⁻1
11. ⁻3 + 7 = 4
12. 5 + 2 = 7

Page 95

13. 1
14. 48
15. ⁻8
16. ⁻8
17. 17
18. 144
19. ⁻30
20. 12
21. 325
22. ⁻198
23. 63
24. 85
25. ⁻5080
26. 22
27. ⁻1120
28. ⁻8
29. ⁻12
30. ⁻126
31. ⁻2
32. 3
33. ⁻3
34. 25
35. 81
36. ⁻3

TEST PREP ANSWERS
Page 96

1. B
2. H
3. A
4. J
5. E
6. H
7. E
8. J
9. B
10. H

Name _____   Date _____

Order of Operations

We need to be sure that everyone gets the same answer to a problem. So we agree to use the order of operations. Parentheses are used to change the order in which operations are done.

Order of Operations
1. Work inside parentheses.
2. Find the value of powers (exponents) and roots.
3. Multiply and divide from left to right.
4. Add and subtract from left to right.

213-214 Find the value of each expression. Show each step.

$16 + 8 \div 4 - 3 =$
$16 + \quad 2 \quad - 3 =$
$\quad 18 \quad - 3 = 15$

$(16 + 8) \div 4 - 3 =$
$\quad 24 \quad \div 4 - 3 =$
$\quad 6 \quad - 3 = 3$

1. $5 \times 2 + 9 =$ **2.** $5 \times (2 + 9) =$ **3.** $(2 + 3)^2 =$ **4.** $2^2 + 3^2 =$

= _____   = _____   = _____   = _____

5. $9 - (2 \times 4) =$ **6.** $(9 - 2) \times 4 =$ **7.** $12 \div 3 - 2 =$ **8.** $12 \div (3 - 2) =$

= _____   = _____   = _____   = _____

9. $(19 - 2) \times 5 + 3 =$ **10.** $19 - (2 \times 5) + 3 =$ **11.** $19 - 2 \times (5 + 3) =$

= _____   = _____   = _____

12. $2 \times (9 - 4)^2 =$ **13.** $(2 \times 9) - 4^2 =$ **14.** $(2 \times 9 - 4)^2 =$

= _____   = _____   = _____

Insert parentheses to make each number sentence true.

15. $16 \div 4 + 4 \times 3 = 6$ **16.** $5 - 3 \times 2 + 7 = 6$ **17.** $36 \div 6 \times 2 + 4 = 7$

Name _____ Date _____

Order of Operations

Directions: For each problem, write a number sentence showing the order of operations and compute to find the answer.

1. In an apple orchard, 4 friends picked 3 bags of apples each and 5 extra apples. Each bag holds 10 apples. How many apples did the friends pick in all?

2. On Saturday, 5 girls held a car wash to earn money. For each car, they charged $6.00. The girls washed a total of 22 cars and collected an extra $10.00 in tips. If they divide the money equally, how much will each girl receive?

3. Nico bought 4 gallons of paint at $15.00 per gallon and 3 quarts of stain at $9.00 per quart. Including a tax of $4.35, what was the total cost?

4. A mini-van holds 8 students. For a field trip, the school provided 6 mini-vans. Every mini-van was full, but at the last minute, 2 students decided not to go. How many students went on the field trip?

5. At the fair, 3 boys were selling fruit smoothies for $3.50 each. They sold 70 fruit smoothies and collected $7.00 in tips. If they divide the money equally, how much will each boy receive?

6. Gretchen bought 50 calendars for $2.50 each and sold them for $4.00 each. How much profit did she make?

PRACTICE ANSWERS
Page 98

1. 19
2. 55
3. 25
4. 13
5. 1
6. 28
7. 2
8. 12
9. 88
10. 12
11. 136
12. 50
13. 2
14. 196
15. $16 \div (4 + 4) \times 3 = 6$
16. $5 - (3 \times 2) + 7 = 6$
17. $36 \div (6 \times 2) + 4 = 7$

TEST PREP ANSWERS
Page 99

1. $4 \times (3 \times 10) + 5 = 125$ apples
2. $(22 \times \$6.00) + \$10.00 \div 5 = \$28.40$
3. $(4 \times \$15.00) + (3 \times \$9.00) + \$4.35 = \$91.35$
4. $(8 \times 6) - 2 = 46$ students
5. $(70 \times \$3.50) + \$7.00 \div 3 = \$84.00$
6. $50 \times (\$4.00 - \$2.50) = \$75.00$

Name _____ Date _____

Properties

The properties of numbers are true for all numbers.
You can use properties to help explain why your thinking is correct.

Property	Example
Commutative Property of Addition You can add two numbers in either order without changing the answer.	$17 + (19 + 23) = 17 + (23 + 19)$
Associative Property of Addition When adding three or more numbers, you can group any pair of numbers together and add them first.	$17 + (23 + 19) = (17 + 23) + 19$
Commutative Property of Multiplication You can multiply two numbers in either order without changing the answer.	$4 \times (77 \times 25) = 4 \times (25 \times 77)$
Associative Property of Multiplication When multiplying three or more numbers, you can group any pair of them together first and multiply.	$4 \times (25 \times 77) = (4 \times 25) \times 77$
Distributive Property When a number is written as a sum or difference of two numbers, you can multiply it by multiplying the entire number or by multiplying each part and adding or subtracting.	$26 \times 7 + 26 \times 3 = 26 \times (7 + 3)$ $7 \times (11 - 4) = (7 \times 11) - (7 \times 4)$

Write the name of the number property that explains why
each number sentence is true.

217-226

1. $(33 \times 8) \times 5 = 33 \times (8 \times 5)$ 2. $(16 \times 9) \times 5 = (9 \times 16) \times 5$

_____   _____

3. $(\frac{1}{6} + \frac{3}{4}) + \frac{5}{6} = (\frac{3}{4} + \frac{1}{6}) + \frac{5}{6}$ 4. $(\frac{3}{4} + \frac{1}{6}) + \frac{5}{6} = \frac{3}{4} + (\frac{1}{6} + \frac{5}{6})$

_____   _____

5. $40 \times (100 - 5) = 40 \times 100 - 40 \times 5$ 6. $11 \times 6 + 11 \times 14 = 11 \times (6 + 14)$

_____   _____

7. $20 \times (5 \times 48) = (20 \times 5) \times 48$ 8. $(4 + \frac{1}{2}) \times \frac{1}{4} = 4 \times \frac{1}{4} + \frac{1}{2} \times \frac{1}{4}$

_____   _____

9. $(8.6 + 9.7) + 1.3 = 8.6 + (9.7 + 1.3)$ 10. $45 \times (200 - 2) = 45 \times 200 - 45 \times 2$

_____   _____

Name _____ Date _____

Five more number properties (other than the commutative, associative, and distributive properties), and two properties of equality are shown below.

Number Properties	Equality Properties
Identity Element for Addition The sum of any number and 0 is that same number.	**Addition Property of Equality** When you have an equation, you can add the same number to each side, and the sides will still be equal.
Identity Element for Multiplication The product of any number and 1 is that same number.	**Multiplication Property of Equality** When you have an equation, you can multiply each side by the same number, and the sides will still be equal.
Additive Inverse Every number has an opposite.	
Multiplicative Inverse Every number except 0 has a reciprocal.	
Zero Property The product of any number and 0 is 0.	

227-234

You can use these properties to solve equations. Try to get the variable alone on one side of the equation. Write the property that explains why each step is true.

$$3x = 36$$

$\frac{1}{3} \times (3x) = \frac{1}{3} \times 36$ Multiplication Property of Equality

$(\frac{1}{3} \times 3) \times x = \frac{1}{3} \times 36$ **11.** _____

$1 \times x = \frac{1}{3} \times 36$ **12.** _____

$1 \times x = 12$ Multiplication fact

$x = 12$ **13.** _____

The steps for solving the equation are shown.
Write the property that explains why each step is true.

$$w + 9 = 35$$

$(w + 9) - 9 = 35 - 9$ **14.** _____

$w + (9 - 9) = 35 - 9$ **15.** _____

$w + 0 = 35 - 9$ **16.** _____

$w + 0 = 26$ Subtraction fact

$w = 26$ **17.** _____

Name _____ Date _____

Properties

Directions: Answer each question using numbers, words, or pictures.

1 What number belongs in the boxes to make BOTH number sentences true?

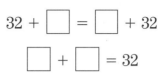

$$32 + \boxed{} = \boxed{} + 32$$

$$\boxed{} + \boxed{} = 32$$

2 Meryl was trying to compute $4 \times 12 \times 5$.
Jack told her that the answer is 20×12, or 240. Is Jack correct? Explain.

3 Hannah has 42 balloons for a party. Her mom gives her 3 more balloons. If Hannah shares the balloons equally among 9 children, how many balloons will each child get? Show your work.

4 Clark wrote these number sentences. Are they correct? Explain.

$$6 \times 1 = 6 \qquad\qquad 1 \div 6 = 6$$

5 What number belongs in the boxes to make BOTH number sentences true?

$$\boxed{} \times \tfrac{1}{7} = 1 \qquad\qquad \boxed{} + {}^{-}7 = 0$$

Math at Hand

PRACTICE ANSWERS
Page 101

1. Associative Property of Multiplication
2. Commutative Property of Multiplication
3. Commutative Property of Addition
4. Associative Property of Addition
5. Distributive Property
6. Distributive Property
7. Associative Property of Multiplication
8. Distributive Property
9. Associative Property of Addition
10. Distributive Property

Page 102

11. Associative Property of Multiplication
12. Multiplicative Inverse
13. Identity Element for Multiplication
14. Addition Property of Equality
15. Associative Property of Addition
16. Additive Inverse
17. Identity Element for Addition

TEST PREP ANSWERS
Page 103

1. 16
2. Yes. $4 \times 12 \times 5$ is the same as $4 \times 5 \times 12$, which is 20×12, or 240. This shows the Associative Property of Multiplication.
3. $(42 + 3) \div 9 = 45 \times \frac{1}{9}$ $= \frac{45}{9} = 5$ balloons
4. No. One is the Identity Element for Multiplication but not for division. So $6 \times 1 = 6$ is correct, but $1 \div 6 = \frac{1}{6}$, not 6.
5. 7

Name _____ Date _____

Expressions and Equations

When you have equal-size groups, you can use a variable to represent the size of the groups. Then you can write expressions for word problems.

Let b = the number of people seated on a full city bus.

Word expression	Algebraic expression for number of people seated
5 people stand up ⟶	$b - 5$
5 people put children on their laps ⟶	$b + 5$
5 busloads of people ⟶	$5 \times b$, or $5 \bullet b$, or $5b$
Equal groups go to 5 places ⟶	$b \div 5$, or $\frac{b}{5}$

Write an algebraic expression for each word expression.   238

1. A number m increased by 4   **2.** A number q minus 10

_____   _____

3. 17 times a number g **4.** A number x divided into 6 equal groups

_____   _____

5. 8 less than a number d **6.** 20 more than a number s

_____   _____

Evaluate each expression.   239, 246

$4 \times n$ for $n = 14$ $l \bullet w$ for $l = 7$ and $w = 12$

$4 \times n = 4 \times 14 = 56$ $l \bullet w = 7 \bullet 12 = 84$

7. $t \div 6$ for $t = 72$ _____   **8.** $k + 15$ for $k = 25$ _____

9. $6h$ for $h = 9$ _____   **10.** s^2 for $s = 8$ _____

11. $d^2 + 3$ for $d = 4$ _____   **12.** $5x - 7$ for $x = 4$ _____

13. $B \bullet h$ for $B = 12, h = 2$ _____   **14.** $2l + 2w$ for $l = 6, w = 5$ _____

15. $r \bullet t$ for $r = 40, t = 3$ _____   **16.** $\frac{1}{2}bh$ for $b = 6, h = 3$ _____

17. s^2h for $s = 9, h = 10$ _____   **18.** $\frac{9}{5}t + 32$ for $t = 25$ _____

Name _____ Date _____

To solve addition and subtraction equations, think about missing addends and sums. Check your solutions by substituting them back into the equation. Then see if the equation is true.

$k + 9 = 23$	$p - 12 = 29$
Think: What number can I add to 9 to get 23? Since $23 - 9 = 14$, then $14 + 9 = 23$. So $k = 14$.	**Think:** From what number can I subtract 12 to get 29? Since $29 + 12 = 41$, then $41 - 12 = 29$. So $p = 41$.
Check: Substitute into the original equation: $k + 9 = 14 + 9 = 23$. The solution checks.	**Check:** Substitute into the original equation: $p - 12 = 41 - 12 = 29$. The solution checks.

242   Solve each addition or subtraction equation. Check each solution.

19. $x + 7 = 19$ **20.** $y - 8 = 12$ **21.** $8 + g = 19$

Solution: _____   Solution _____   Solution _____

Check _____   Check _____   Check _____

22. $r + 68 = 292$ **23.** $v - 56 = 85$ **24.** $116 - w = 95$

Solution: _____   Solution _____   Solution _____

Check _____   Check _____   Check _____

$5z = 95$	$\frac{t}{35} = 6$
Think: How many fives are in 95? $95 \div 5 = 19$. So $z = 19$.	**Think:** What number can I divide by 35 to get 6? $35 \times 6 = 210$. So $t = 210$.
Check: $5z = 5 \cdot 19 = 95$	**Check:** $\frac{t}{35} = \frac{210}{35} = 210 \div 35 = 6$

243   Solve each multiplication or division equation. Check each solution.

25. $23t = 207$ **26.** $15h = 255$ **27.** $\frac{168}{e} = 14$

Solution: _____   Solution _____   Solution _____

Check _____   Check _____   Check _____

28. $\frac{d}{15} = 11$ **29.** $8m = 104$ **30.** $\frac{225}{s} = 9$

Solution: _____   Solution _____   Solution _____

Check _____   Check _____   Check _____

Name _____ Date _____

Some equations have more than one variable. Then they can have many solutions. You can make a table of values to find a few of them.

Graph the solutions to the equation $y = 2x$.

| First make a table of values. | List the ordered pairs from the table. | Plot the points. Join the points with a line to show all solutions. |

x	$y = 2x$
0	0
1	2
2	4
3	6
4	8

Ordered pairs
(0, 0)
(1, 2)
(2, 4)
(3, 6)
(4, 8)

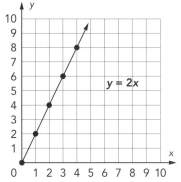

Make a table of values for each equation.
Then graph each one.

31. $y = x + 2$

x	$y = x + 2$
0	
1	
2	
3	
4	

32. $y = x - 3$

x	$y = x - 3$
3	
4	
5	
6	
7	

33. $y = \frac{x}{3}$

x	$y = \frac{x}{3}$
0	
3	
6	
9	

34. $y = 1.5x$

x	$y = 1.5x$
0	
2	
4	
6	

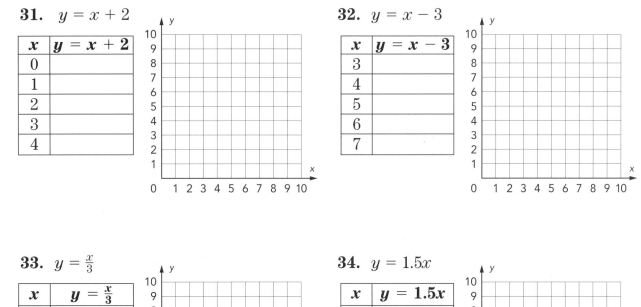
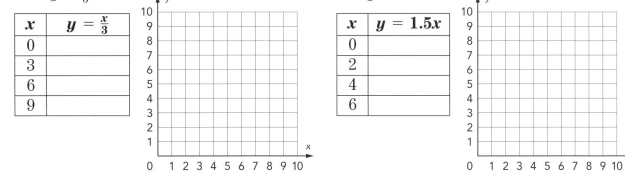

Name _____ Date _____

Expressions and Equations

Directions: Write the answer to each question.

(1) Theo has *n* baseball cards in his collection. Lenny has twice as many cards as Theo. Write an expression that represents the total number of cards in Theo and Lenny's collections.

(2) Mrs. Janus has 18 students in her class. She has to give each student 3 workbooks. Write and solve an equation to find the total number of workbooks she needs.

(3) Pete bought 4 dozen eggs, but 5 of the eggs were broken when he got home. Write and solve an equation to find how many eggs he had left.

(4) Mack made 192 greeting cards to sell at the craft fair. He put an equal number of cards in each of 16 boxes. Write and solve an equation to find how many cards he put in each box.

(5) Diego built a rectangular patio 32 feet long and 20 feet wide. What is the area of the patio? (Use $A = lw$.)

(6) Rosa was making a wall 32 feet long. She had 2-foot blocks and 4-foot blocks. For each row, she could use no more than 12 blocks. How many different combinations of 2-foot blocks and 4-foot blocks could she use in one row? Write an equation to solve the problem. Then fill in the table of values and plot the points on the graph.

2-ft	4-ft

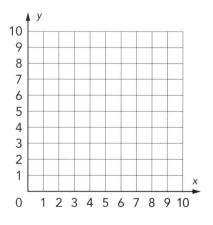

PRACTICE ANSWERS
Page 105

1. $m + 4$
2. $q - 10$
3. $17 \times g$, or $17g$
4. $x \div 6$, or $\frac{x}{6}$
5. $d - 8$
6. $s + 20$
7. 12
8. 40
9. 54
10. 64
11. 19
12. 13
13. 24
14. 22
15. 120
16. 9
17. 810
18. 77

Page 106

19. $x = 12; 12 + 7 = 19$
20. $y = 20; 20 - 8 = 12$
21. $g = 11; 8 + 11 = 19$
22. $r = 224; 224 + 68 = 292$
23. $v = 141; 141 - 56 = 85$
24. $w = 21; 116 - 21 = 95$
25. $t = 9; 23 \times 9 = 207$
26. $h = 17; 15 \times 17 = 255$
27. $e = 12; 168 \div 12 = 14$
28. $d = 165; 165 \div 15 = 11$
29. $m = 13; 8 \times 13 = 104$
30. $s = 25; 225 \div 25 = 9$

Page 107

31. Table values: 2, 3, 4, 5, 6

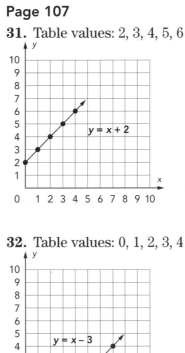

32. Table values: 0, 1, 2, 3, 4

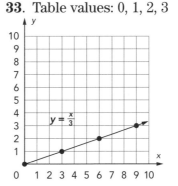

33. Table values: 0, 1, 2, 3

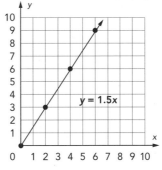

34. Table values: 0, 3, 6, 9

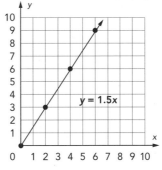

TEST PREP ANSWERS
Page 108

1. $n + 2n$
2. $w = 18 \times 3;$
   $w = 54$ workbooks
3. $e = (4 \times 12) - 5;$
   $e = 43$ eggs
4. $c = 192 \div 16$, or
   $\frac{192}{c} = 16; c = 12$ cards
5. $A = 32$ ft $\times 20$ ft;
   $A = 640$ sq ft
6. $2a + 4b = 32$

a	b
2	7
4	6
6	5
8	4

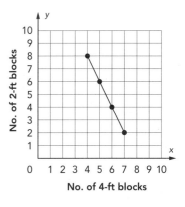

Party Express

TIME
• 45–60 minutes

OBJECTIVE
• Write and evaluate algebraic expressions

MATERIALS
• Math Notebook Page, page 190

TEACHER NOTES
• Make sure students understand the meaning of the word "per" and know the total number of adults and children involved in Patrick's party before they begin writing expressions.

• Have the students read their word expressions and identify a key letter that could be used as a variable. The next step would be to replace the word with the variable.

EXTENSIONS
• Use the activity to present a lesson about the fine art of budgeting and determining a per unit cost.

• Have the students plan a class party using costs from local locations. Have them use algebraic expressions to figure out the total cost for the class.

• Students can use variables and expressions to figure out the cost of having their own parties at home. Include such things as food, hats, games, and so on.

• Use travel advertisements from your local paper to calculate the cost of taking a trip. Students might write a story about the trip and use three elements from the story that can be written in the form of an expression using variables.

ANSWERS

1.

Cost per person	$3.00
Write a word expression for the total cost	$3.00 times the no. of people
Write an algebraic expression for the total cost	$3.00p
Total cost:	$39.00

2.

Admission cost per person for adults	$2.50
Write a word expression	$2.50 times the number of **a**dults
Write an algebraic expression	$2.50 **a**
Total admission cost for adults:	$5.00
Admission cost per person for children	$0.50
Write a word expression	$0.50 times the number of **c**hildren
Write an algebraic expression	$0.50 **c**
Total admission cost for children:	$5.50
Cost per person for a meal	$2.50
Write a word expression	$2.50 times the number of **p**eople
Write an algebraic expression	$2.50 **p**
Total cost for meals:	$32.50
Add the totals	Total cost for the party: $43.00

3. Answers will vary. You may want to point out that the cost may not be the only deciding factor, especially since the costs for the parties are so close. Read students' explanations for reasonableness, and to check that they have used the information in the charts.

Name _____ Date _____

Expressions and
  Equations: 235

Variables and
  Constants: 236

Expressions: 237

Writing Expressions:
  238

Evaluating Expressions:
  239

HANDBOOK HELP

Party Express

Patrick wants to have a special party for his eleventh birthday and invite ten of his classmates. He wants to take them to play miniature golf or to the local zoo. He tells his parents about his ideas. They say they will be happy to drive the children and provide supervision, but they want Patrick to figure out how each idea will cost before they agree to the party. Patrick quickly gets on the telephone and calls the Fun Golf and the local zoo. Both places have special rates for parties. Patrick's notes are scribbled below. Complete the questions to help Patrick figure out how much each party will cost.

1. Use the information from Fun Golf to complete the chart below.

Cost per person	
Write a word expression for the total cost	
Write an algebraic expression for the total cost	
Total cost:	

FUN GOLF

- $3.00 per person
- 18 holes, 3 different courses
- for parties, price includes 2 slices of pizza and a small drink

2. Use the information from the zoo to complete the chart below.

Admission cost per person for adults	
Write a word expression	
Write an algebraic expression	
Total admission cost for adults:	
Admission cost per person for children	
Write a word expression	
Write an algebraic expression	
Total admission cost for children:	
Cost per person for a meal	
Write a word expression	
Write an algebraic expression	
Total cost for meals:	
Add the totals	Total cost for the party:

ZOO

- admission is $2.50 for adults, $0.50 for children under 13
- for parties, a hot dog, chips, small drink for $2.50 per person

3. On your Math Notebook Page, use the information in the charts and write a brief explanation of which party you would choose and why. Be sure to include information on the cost involved.

Name _____ Date _____

Gathering Data

253-254 What letters are used most often in the English language? To find the answer, you can take a writing sample and count how many times each letter occurs. Usually a longer sample will give results more like the whole language than a shorter sample. For example, in a short sample such as "Beekeepers never sneeze" the letter *z* is more common than any of the vowels *a*, *i*, *o*, or *u*!

1. Use the poem at the right. Complete the table below by tallying how many times each letter occurs.

Letter	Tally	Letter	Tally
a		n	
b		o	
c		p	
d		q	
e		r	
f		s	
g		t	
h		u	
i		v	
j		w	
k		x	
l		y	
m		z	

I never saw a purple cow.
I never hope to see one.
But I can tell you anyhow
I'd rather see than be one!

2. What letter appears most often? _____

3. What two letters appear second most often? _____

4. What letters do not appear at all? _____

5. In English, the most frequently used letters are *e, t, a,* and *o*. How do your results compare?

_____

6. Why do you think your results are different? _____

_____

Name _____ Date _____

Gathering Data

1. Suppose your school serves five different hot lunches each week: pizza, macaroni and cheese, hamburgers, grilled cheese, and chicken pot pie. How would you find out which lunches are most popular among your classmates? Explain how you would collect data to answer this question and make a table showing how you would record the data.

2. For a science project, you must record the outside temperature at 7:00 A.M. and 6:00 P.M. each day for one week. Make a table that you could use to record the data.

PRACTICE ANSWERS
Page 112

1.

Letter	Tally
a	HH I
b	II
c	II
d	I
e	HH HH HH
f	
g	
h	IIII
i	IIII
j	
k	
l	III
m	
n	HH II
o	HH II
p	III
q	
r	HH
s	III
t	HH
u	III
v	II
w	III
x	
y	II
z	

2. e
3. n and o
4. f, g, j, k, m, q, x, and z
5. The vowels occur about as often, but in this sample, n appeared more often than t.
6. Answers will vary. Possible answer: The sample size was small.

TEST PREP ANSWERS
Page 113

1. Ask each student in the class what his or her favorite lunch is. Keep a tally of which lunch each person chooses.

Favorite Lunch	Number of Students
pizza	
macaroni and cheese	
hamburgers	
grilled cheese	
chicken pot pie	

2.

Temperatures		
Day	7:00 A.M.	6:00 P.M.
Sunday		
Monday		
Tuesday		
Wednesday		
Thursday		
Friday		
Saturday		

Name _____ Date _____

Summarizing Data with Statistics

The number of students in each classroom at Elmwood School is shown in the table at the right.

Class Sizes at Elmwood School				
Grade	Number in Each Classroom			
K	17	17	18	19
1	21	21	21	
2	19	20	20	
3	23	23	11	
4	25	23	12	

The range of the data is the difference between the greatest and least numbers in the data. For these classroom sizes it is:
Range = 25 − 11 = 14.

The outliers are any numbers that are much greater or less than the others. For this data the outliers are 11 and 12. You can use the range and the outliers to describe the data in two ways.

ONE WAY The range of the class sizes is 14 students.

ANOTHER WAY The range of most class sizes is 8 students, although 2 classes are much smaller than this.

Using any outliers along with the range gives a much clearer picture of the data.

Video Games Played Today	
Alma	1
Belinda	0
Cedrick	3
Eddy	4
Fran	15
Gina	2
Herold	3

 256-258

Use the data at the right to answer questions 1–4.

1. What is the range of the data? _____ games

2. Does the data have an outlier? If so, what is it?

_____

Write two descriptions of the data using the range and any outlier.

3. _____

4. _____

Use the data at the right to answer questions 5–8.

Number of Commercials		
Time Slot	Station X	Station Y
7:00–7:30 P.M.	19	12
7:30–8:00 P.M.	20	19
8:00–8:30 P.M.	22	21
8:30–9:00 P.M.	19	22

5. What is the range of the data? _____

6. What is the outlier? _____

Describe the data two ways using the range and the outlier.

7. _____

8. _____

Name _____ Date _____

A company sells many styles of 4-person tents. The prices are shown at the right. The typical or average price of the tents can be found in three ways.

Prices of 4-Person Tents
$179 $279 $169 $199 $189

ONE WAY Use the **mean**. This is the sum of the items divided by the number of items.

$$(179 + 279 + 169 + 199 + 189) \div 5 = 1015 \div 5 = \$203$$

ANOTHER WAY Use the **median**. This is the middle number when the data are listed in order from least to greatest. If there are two middle numbers, find the mean of the two numbers.

169   **179**   **189**   **199**   **179**

ANOTHER WAY Use the **mode**. It is the number that appears most often. If no number occurs more often than the others, there is no mode.

The data for the prices of the tents has no mode.

Notice that 4 of the 5 prices are less than the mean. The mean is not typical of this set of data. The median of $189 is a better price to use to describe the typical or average price of a 4-person tent.

004-005 Find the typical or average price for each item.

9. What is the mean? _____

Prices of Backpacks
$139 $129 $119 $49 $55 $55

10. What is the median? _____   11. What is the mode?_____

12. What is a typical or average price for a backpack? Explain you choice.

_____

_____

Prices of Hiking Boots
$75 $109 $75 $89 $99 $99 $149 $85

13. What is the mean? _____

14. What is the median? _____   15. What is the mode? _____

16. What is a typical or average price for a backpack? Explain you choice.

_____

_____

Name _____ Date _____

Summarizing Data with Statistics

Directions: Eight students competed in a geography contest. The students got points for each question answered correctly. The table below shows the points earned by each student. Use the table to answer the questions below. Show your work.

Geography Contest	
Student	**Score**
Greg	265
Valerie	245
Susan	280
Charles	320
Stacey	290
Frank	250
Lena	280
Keith	270

1. Find the range of the data.

2. Find the mean score.

3. Find the median score.

4. Find the mode.

PRACTICE ANSWERS
Page 115

1. 15 games
2. 15 games
3. The range of the number of games played is 15.
4. The range of most of the games played is 4, but one person played many more games than that.
5. 10 commercials
6. 12 commercials
7. The range of the number of commercials is 10.
8. The range of most of the commercials is 3, but one time slot had many less commercials than that.

Page 116

9. $91
10. $87
11. $55
12. Answers will vary. Possible answer: Either $91 or $87, because the mode is much too low to be typical.
13. $97.50
14. $94
15. The prices are bimodal. There are two pairs of boots that sell for $75 and two that sell for $99.
16. The mean and median prices are very close to each other, and are good typical prices. The higher of the two modes ($99) fits well with the mean and the median as a typical price.

TEST PREP ANSWERS
Page 117

1. $320 - 245 = 75$
2. $2200 \div 8 = 275$
3. $270 + 280 = 550 \div 2 = 275$
4. 280

Name _____ Date _____

Displaying Data

In the 1998 Winter Olympics, five of the highest scoring countries were Germany (29 medals), Norway (25 medals), Russia (18 medals), Canada (15 medals), and the United States (13 medals).

1. Make a single-bar graph of this data. Be sure to label the scales.

275, 273

2. The United States won 6 gold medals, 3 silver medals, and 4 bronze medals. Make a circle graph of this data. The outside of the circle is marked off into 13 equal sections to help you.

274, 276

3. Which country won about twice as many medals in all as the U.S. team?

   _____

4. Which graph did you use? _____

5. About half of the U.S. medals were of which type? _____

6. Which graph did you use? _____

Name _____   Date _____

278

7. Use the data below. At the right, make a single-line graph of the data.

U.S. Population	
Year	(in millions)
1980	225
1990	250
2000	275
2010	300
2050	400

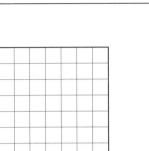

8. Is the population increasing, decreasing, or neither? _____

9. How can you tell from the graph? _____

280 The two largest cities in the U.S.—New York City and Los Angeles—grew very differently during the last half-century.

10. Use the data below. Make a double-line graph of the data.

Population (in millions)		
Year	Los Angeles	New York City
1950	1.9	7.9
1970	2.8	7.9
1980	3.0	7.0
1990	3.5	7.3
1996	3.5	7.4

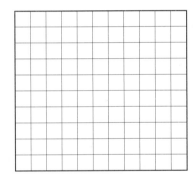

11. During which period of time did the population of New York City decline? _____

Your grandmother gave you this list to show you how much new technology has appeared in her lifetime. The dates show the years when she first remembers using or owning the new inventions.

12. Make a time line of the information below.

Year	Event
1925	She was born.
1932	First "talkie" movie
1935	First radio
1948	First telephone
1950	First washing machine
1954	First television
1965	First airplane trip
1982	First microwave oven
1994	First computer

Name _____ Date _____

Mr. Zina's class wanted to find out how many CDs their classmates owned. They took a survey and got the following results:

12, 23, 19, 30, 8, 17, 14, 24, 17, 25, 19, 15, 14, 24, 12, 25, 20, 14, 25, 13

Yoko thought the best way to see the data would be to make a line plot.

282

13. Use the data to make a line plot below.

8　10　12　14　16　18　20　22　24　26　28　30

Dwight suggested they could use a stem-and-leaf plot to see the data.

284

14. Use the data to make a stem-and-leaf plot below. Use the two steps shown.

First place all the data in the order in which they appear

Then arrange the leaves in order from least to greatest.

0	
1	
2	
3	

0	
1	
2	
3	

15. What is the range of the data? _____ **16.** What is the mode? _____

17. How many items of data are there? _____ **18.** What is the median? _____

The Venn diagram at the right shows which students have CDs and cassettes at home.

283

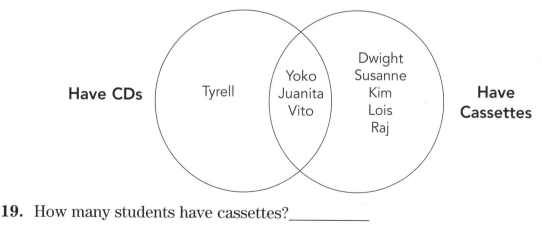

Have CDs　　Tyrell　　Yoko Juanita Vito　　Dwight Susanne Kim Lois Raj　　**Have Cassettes**

19. How many students have cassettes? _____

20. How many students have both cassettes and CDs? _____

Name _____ Date _____

Displaying Data

Directions: Each question below gives a set of data. On a separate piece of paper, make a graph to display the data for each question.

1. LaToya made a table showing how much of her allowance she spent on different things in the month of April. Make a circle graph to show these data. Be sure to label each part and include a title.

Clothes	30%
Food	20%
Entertainment	25%
Books and CDs	10%
School Supplies	15%

2. The Moretown Blades hockey team plays 60 games each season. The table below shows how many games they won each season. Make a bar graph to display these data.

Season	Wins
1996	36
1997	25
1998	48
1999	40
2000	55

3. During a hurricane in Charleston, a computer recorded the changes in wind speed every two hours. Make a line graph to display these data.

Time	Wind Speed (knots/hr)
8:00 A.M.	65
10:00 A.M.	80
12:00 NOON	85
2:00 P.M.	105
4:00 P.M.	90
6:00 P.M.	54

4. The manager of a convenience store did a study to find how much money his customers spent per visit. Make a line plot to show the spread of these data.

Amounts Spent by Customers			
$12	$24	$10	$12
$6	$18	$15	$15
$10	$12	$22	$16
$8	$8	$18	$12
$10	$7	$16	$10

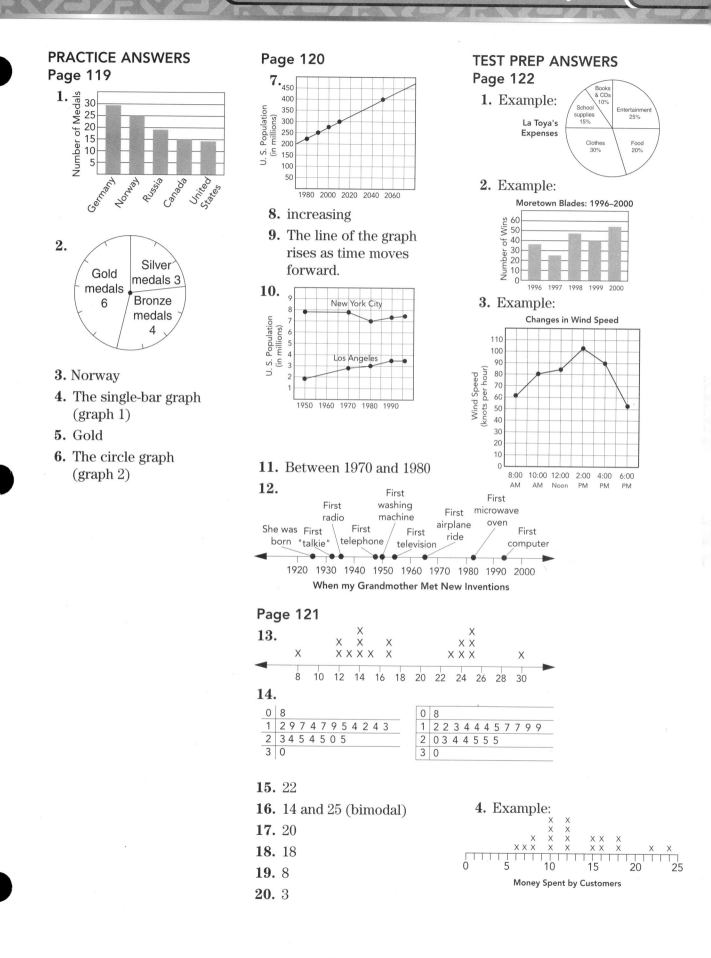

PRACTICE ANSWERS
Page 119

1. Number of Medals bar graph (Germany, Norway, Russia, Canada, United States)

2. Circle graph: Gold medals 6, Silver medals 3, Bronze medals 4

3. Norway

4. The single-bar graph (graph 1)

5. Gold

6. The circle graph (graph 2)

Page 120

7. U.S. Population (in millions) line graph, 1980–2060

8. increasing

9. The line of the graph rises as time moves forward.

10. U.S. Population (in millions) — New York City and Los Angeles, 1950–1990

11. Between 1970 and 1980

12. When my Grandmother Met New Inventions timeline: She was born, First "talkie", First radio, First telephone, First washing machine, First television, First airplane ride, First microwave oven, First computer (1920–2000)

Page 121

13. Line plot (X marks) from 8 to 30

14. Stem-and-leaf plots

0	8
1	2 9 7 4 7 9 5 4 2 4 3
2	3 4 5 4 5 0 5
3	0

0	8
1	2 2 3 4 4 4 5 7 7 9 9
2	0 3 4 4 5 5 5
3	0

15. 22

16. 14 and 25 (bimodal)

17. 20

18. 18

19. 8

20. 3

TEST PREP ANSWERS
Page 122

1. Example: La Toya's Expenses circle graph — School supplies 15%, Books & CDs 10%, Entertainment 25%, Food 20%, Clothes 30%

2. Example: Moretown Blades: 1996–2000 bar graph, Number of Wins, 1996–2000

3. Example: Changes in Wind Speed line graph, Wind Speed (knots per hour), 8:00 AM–6:00 PM

4. Example: Money Spent by Customers line plot (X marks) from 0 to 25

Name _____ Date _____

Probability

To calculate the probability of an event, you must find the ratio of favorable outcomes to all possible outcomes.

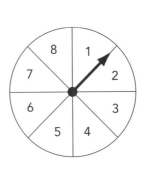

Find the probability of spinning a 3 on the spinner at the right.

There are 8 equally likely outcomes for this spinner: 1, 2, 3, 4, 5, 6, 7, and 8. Only one of these numbers is a favorable outcome— 3.

So, $P(3) = \dfrac{\text{favorable outcomes}}{\text{possible outcomes}} = \dfrac{1}{8}$

Find the probability of spinning an even number on the same spinner.

There are still 8 possible outcomes, but now 4 of them are favorable: 2, 4, 6 or 8.

So, $P(\text{even number}) = \dfrac{4}{8}$ or $\dfrac{1}{2}$

286-288 Use the spinner above to answer questions 1–5. What is the probability of spinning

1. a 2 or a 3?
   Favorable outcomes: _____ and _____ $P(2 \text{ or } 3) =$ _____

2. an odd number?
   Favorable outcomes: _____ $P(\text{odd number}) =$ _____

3. a multiple of 3?
   Favorable outcomes: _____ $P(\text{multiple of 3}) =$ _____

4. a number less than 4?
   Favorable outcomes: _____ $P(\text{less than 4}) =$ _____

5. a number less than 10?
   Favorable outcomes: _____ $P(\text{less than 10}) =$ _____

286-287 Find the probability of spinning each letter or group of letters on the spinner at the right. Each section of the spinner is equally likely.

6. $P(A) =$ _____   7. $P(B) =$ _____

8. $P(C) =$ _____   9. $P(B \text{ or } C) =$ _____

10. $P(Z) =$ _____   11. $P(A \text{ or } C) =$ _____

Name _____ Date _____

Papa's Pizza gives you a choice of two crusts—regular or extra crispy—
and 5 toppings—cheese, pepperoni, sausage, peppers, and mushrooms.
How many different pizzas does Papa's Pizza make?

ONE WAY You can make a tree diagram to list all the possibilities.

regular ⟨ cheese, sausage, pepperoni, peppers, mushroom

extra crispy ⟨ cheese, sausage, pepperoni, peppers, mushroom

ANOTHER WAY Or you can use the counting principle:

Number of different pizzas = Number of crusts × Number of toppings
= 2 × 5
= 10 different pizzas

Solve each problem.

291-292

12. A store sells one style of T-shirt in three colors—
black, blue, and white. It is available in three
sizes—small, medium, and large. Make a tree
diagram in the space at the right showing all the
choices the store's customers have.

black

13. A sandwich shop offers three choices of bread
and five choices of fillings for its sandwiches.
How many different sandwiches can you buy?

_____

14. A bicycle company makes three styles of bikes,
each available in the same four colors.
How many different bikes can you buy? _____

15. A kite store sells traditional, box,
and dragon-style kites. Each comes
in six colors. How many different
kites are available at the store? _____

16. A fabric company makes spools of thread in three
materials—nylon, cotton, and silk—and in three
spool sizes. Each material and size is available in
50 colors. How many different
thread products does the company sell? _____

Math at Hand

Name _____ Date _____

Probability

Directions: Mark the letter beside the best answer to each question. If your answer is not given, mark the letter beside "Not Here."

1 A spinner is divided into 8 equal parts. If Marie spins once, what is the probability that the spinner will stop on 4?

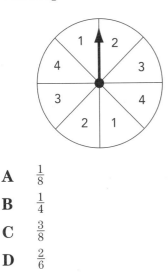

    A $\frac{1}{8}$

    B $\frac{1}{4}$

    C $\frac{3}{8}$

    D $\frac{2}{6}$

2 If Marie spins once, what is the probability that the spinner will land on an odd number?

    F $\frac{1}{2}$

    G $\frac{1}{3}$

    H $\frac{1}{4}$

    J $\frac{3}{8}$

3 If you roll a number cube numbered 1–6, what is the probability that you will roll a 5?

    A $\frac{1}{5}$

    B $\frac{5}{6}$

    C $\frac{1}{3}$

    D $\frac{1}{6}$

4 Jim has 15 white, 3 pink, and 7 yellow golf balls in a bag. If he reaches into the bag and takes out one ball without looking, what is the probability that he will pick a white ball?

    F $\frac{2}{5}$

    G $\frac{10}{15}$

    H $\frac{7}{25}$

    J $\frac{3}{25}$

    K   Not Here

5 Lucy has 5 sweaters and 3 skirts. How many possible combinations of 1 sweater and 1 skirt can she wear?

    A   3

    B   5

    C   8

    D   15

    E   Not Here

6 An ice cream shop offers three flavors: vanilla, chocolate, and strawberry. The customer can have ice cream in a sugar cone or a waffle cone and can have the ice cream plain or with sprinkles. How many possible combinations of flavors and cones are there?

    F   8

    G   12

    H   15

    J   24

    K   Not Here

PRACTICE ANSWERS
Page 124

1. 2 and 3; $\frac{1}{4}$

2. 1, 3, 5, or 7; $\frac{1}{2}$

3. 3 or 6; $\frac{1}{4}$

4. 1, 2, or 3; $\frac{3}{8}$

5. 1, 2, 3, 4, 5, 6, 7, or 8; 1

6. $\frac{1}{6}$

7. $\frac{1}{3}$

8. $\frac{1}{2}$

9. $\frac{5}{6}$

10. 0

11. $\frac{2}{3}$

Page 125

12.

```
black ┬── small
      ├── medium
      └── large

blue  ┬── small
      ├── medium
      └── large

white ┬── small
      ├── medium
      └── large
```

13. 15 sandwiches

14. 12 bikes

15. 18 kites

16. 450 thread products

TEST PREP ANSWERS
Page 126

1. B

2. F

3. D

4. K

5. D

6. G

Gooey Gum Graphs

TIME
• 30–45 minutes

OBJECTIVES
• Understand how data can be presented in a variety of graphs
• Determine the best type of graph to present collected data

MATERIALS
• Gooey Gum Graphs Page, page 191

TEACHER NOTES
• Review gathering and recording data, sample size, and tallies with the students.

• Discuss which type of graph will present the collected information in the clearest way.

EXTENSIONS
• Have students find different types of graphs in newspapers or magazines. Discuss with the class why the type of graph used was chosen to display the collected data.

• This is a good opportunity to discuss whether or not data on a graph is displayed in a misleading manner. Graphs can be misleading for a variety of reasons. If the intervals on the axes are not constant, the data will appear in a distorted way. If there is a large gap between zero and the first number appearing on an axis, the results can appear to be exaggerated. Changing the scale at some point on an axis is another way data can be misrepresented. Try to find some published graphs that present data in a misleading manner.

• Have students conduct their own surveys and display the data in at least two different ways.

• Students can put their data into a spreadsheet program and create an assortment of graphs for the data. Have students discuss which graph makes the data easiest to see at a glance. Make sure the graph they have chosen is appropriate for the data.

ANSWERS
1. 120

2. Graph 1 is a single-bar graph. Graph 2 is a pictograph. Graph 3 is a circle graph. Graph 4 is a single-line graph.

3. 120 is a factor of 360°, so it is easy to show the fractional parts as a whole number of degrees when making the circle graph.

4. Other factors of 360 are 2, 3, 4, 5, 6, 8, 9, 10, 12, 15, 18, 20, 24, 30, 36, 40, 45, 60, 72, 90, and 180. To insure a good sample size, probably 60 or more people should be included in a survey with five choices.

5. Graph 4, the single-line graph, is not a good choice for Janet's data. Single-line graphs are most useful for showing change over time, and time is not an element of Janet's data.

6. Answers will vary. Graphs 1, 2, and 3 make it easy to see which brands of gum are the favorite and the least favorite. Graph 3, the circle graph, also makes it easy to see how the data relate to each other and to the results of the survey as a whole.

Name _____   Date _____

Gooey Gum Graphs

The students in Ms. Park's math class were practicing making graphs. Ms. Park had each student create a survey question, conduct the survey, and make four different graphs displaying the results. Janet decided to take a survey about people's favorite brand of chewing gum. The chart below shows the results of her survey.

The graphs that Janet made are shown on your Gooey Gum Graphs Page. Use the graphs to answer these questions.

1. How many people did Janet include in her survey? _____

2. What four types of graphs did Janet make? _____

_____

Janet chose the number of people she surveyed very carefully. She wanted to make it easy to make Graph 3.

3. Why does the sample size make Graph 3 easy to make?

_____

_____

Favorite Brand of Gum

Brand of Gum	Number of People
Awesome Apple	10
Bodacious Bubble	40
Good-N-Chewy	25
Grand Grape	15
Wild Watermelon	30

4. What other sample sizes could Janet have chosen to make it easy to make Graph 3? Explain why you think so.

_____

_____

5. One type of graph Janet made is not a good choice for displaying the data she has collected. Which graph is that? Explain why it is not a good choice.

_____

_____

6. Which graph do you think makes the results of Janet's survey easy to see at a glance. Explain why you think so.

_____

_____

Name _____   Date _____

Length

To find the perimeter of a figure, add the lengths of all its sides.

Find the perimeter of this figure.

Perimeter = 10 + 10 + 7 + 7 + 16 = 50
The perimeter is 50 in.

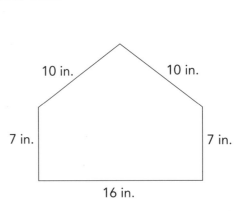

295-297   Find the perimeter of each figure.

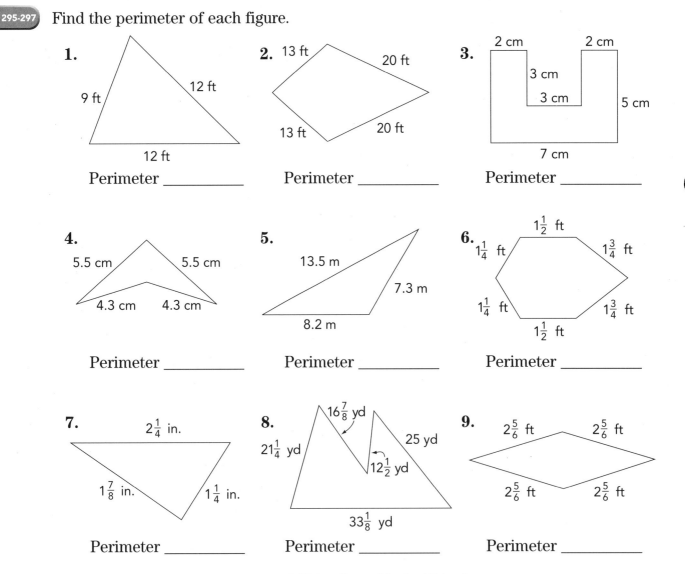

1.
9 ft   12 ft   12 ft

Perimeter _____

2. 13 ft   20 ft   13 ft   20 ft

Perimeter _____

3. 2 cm   2 cm   3 cm   3 cm   5 cm   7 cm

Perimeter _____

4.
5.5 cm   5.5 cm   4.3 cm   4.3 cm

Perimeter _____

5.
13.5 m   7.3 m   8.2 m

Perimeter _____

6. $1\frac{1}{2}$ ft $1\frac{1}{4}$ ft $1\frac{3}{4}$ ft $1\frac{1}{4}$ ft $1\frac{1}{2}$ ft $1\frac{3}{4}$ ft

Perimeter _____

7. $2\frac{1}{4}$ in. $1\frac{7}{8}$ in. $1\frac{1}{4}$ in.

Perimeter _____

8. $16\frac{7}{8}$ yd   25 yd $21\frac{1}{4}$ yd $12\frac{1}{2}$ yd $33\frac{1}{8}$ yd

Perimeter _____

9. $2\frac{5}{6}$ ft $2\frac{5}{6}$ ft $2\frac{5}{6}$ ft $2\frac{5}{6}$ ft

Perimeter _____

10. A triangle has a perimeter of 45 in. One side is 15 in. long and another side is 21 in. long. How long is the third side? _____

Name _____ Date _____

You can use a formula to help you find the perimeter or circumference of a figure.

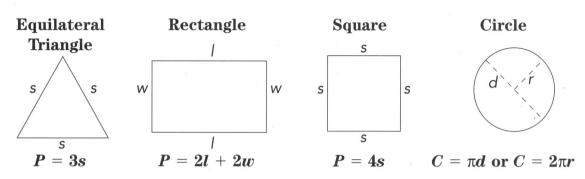

Equilateral Triangle	Rectangle	Square	Circle

$P = 3s$ $P = 2l + 2w$ $P = 4s$ $C = \pi d$ or $C = 2\pi r$

Write the formula for the perimeter or circumference of each figure.
Then calculate it. Use 3.14 as an approximation for π.

296-298

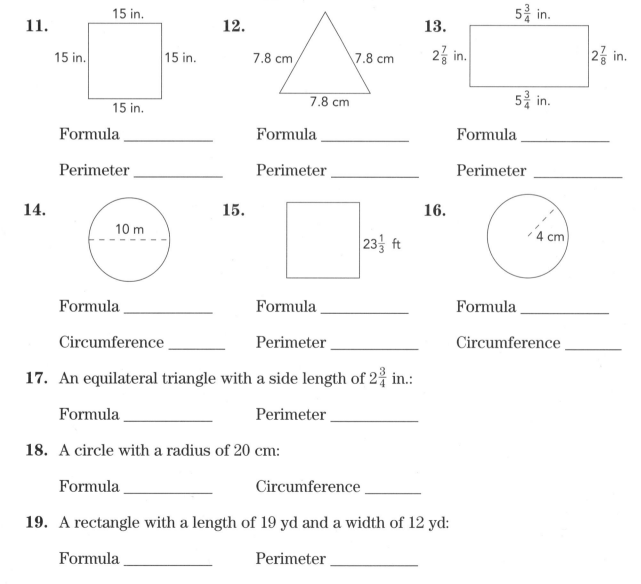

11. 15 in. 15 in. 15 in. 15 in.

Formula _____

Perimeter _____

12. 7.8 cm 7.8 cm 7.8 cm

Formula _____

Perimeter _____

13. $5\frac{3}{4}$ in. $2\frac{7}{8}$ in. $2\frac{7}{8}$ in. $5\frac{3}{4}$ in.

Formula _____

Perimeter _____

14. 10 m

Formula _____

Circumference _____

15. $23\frac{1}{3}$ ft

Formula _____

Perimeter _____

16. 4 cm

Formula _____

Circumference _____

17. An equilateral triangle with a side length of $2\frac{3}{4}$ in.:

Formula _____ Perimeter _____

18. A circle with a radius of 20 cm:

Formula _____ Circumference _____

19. A rectangle with a length of 19 yd and a width of 12 yd:

Formula _____ Perimeter _____

Name _____ Date _____

Length

Directions: Solve each problem. Mark your answer.

1 Mr. Whittaker wants to build a fence around his yard. He measured each side. What is the perimeter?

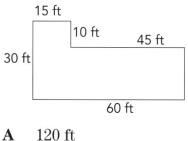

- **A** 120 ft
- **B** 140 ft
- **C** 160 ft
- **D** 180 ft

2 Leslie built a triangular deck. What is the perimeter of the deck?

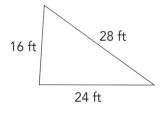

- **F** 34 ft
- **G** 68 ft
- **H** 96 ft
- **J** 176 ft

3 Carmen has a square flower garden that measures 9 m on one side. What is the perimeter of the garden?
- **A** 81 m
- **B** 36 m
- **C** 27 m
- **D** 18 m

4 Gary rides his bike along the streets shown below. How far does he ride?

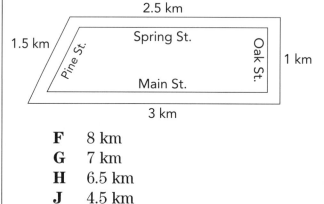

- **F** 8 km
- **G** 7 km
- **H** 6.5 km
- **J** 4.5 km

5 George made a round clock face. What is the circumference of the clock face?

- **A** 30 cm
- **B** 47.1 cm
- **C** 93.2 cm
- **D** 94.2 cm

6 The state house has a round lobby. The diameter of the lobby is 20 yards. What is the circumference of the lobby?
- **F** 6.4 yd
- **G** 60 yd
- **H** 62.8 yd
- **J** 80 yd

PRACTICE ANSWERS
Page 130

1. 33 ft
2. 66 ft
3. 30 cm
4. 19.6 cm
5. 29 m
6. 9 ft
7. $5\frac{3}{8}$ in.
8. $108\frac{3}{4}$ yd
9. $11\frac{1}{3}$ ft
10. 9 in.

Page 131

11. $P = 4s$; 60 in.
12. $P = 3s$; 23.4 cm
13. $P = 2l + 2w$; $17\frac{1}{4}$ in.
14. $C = \pi d$; 31.4 m
15. $P = 4s$; $93\frac{1}{3}$ ft
16. $C = 2\pi r$; 25.12 cm
17. $P = 3s$; $8\frac{1}{4}$ in.
18. $C = 2\pi r$; 125.6 cm
19. $P = 2l + 2w$; 62 yd

TEST PREP ANSWERS
Page 132

1. D
2. G
3. B
4. F
5. D
6. H

Name _____ Date _____

Area

To find the area of a figure, you can count the number of square units within it. Often it is easier to use a formula.

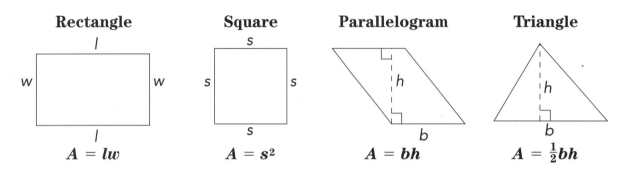

Rectangle	**Square**	**Parallelogram**	**Triangle**
$A = lw$	$A = s^2$	$A = bh$	$A = \frac{1}{2}bh$

301-303 Find the area of each figure.

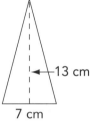

Think: I need to use the formula for a triangle, $A = \frac{1}{2}bh$. The triangle's base is 7 cm, and its height is 13 cm.

$A = \frac{1}{2}bh$

$= \frac{1}{2} \times 7 \times 13$

$= \frac{91}{2}$ or $45\frac{1}{2}$ cm²

1.

5 km

17 km

$A =$ _____

2.

21 mm

35 mm

$A =$ _____

3.

25 mi

25 mi

$A =$ _____

4.

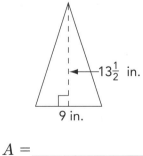

$13\frac{1}{2}$ in.

9 in.

$A =$ _____

5.

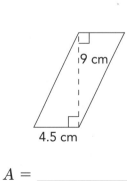

9 cm

4.5 cm

$A =$ _____

6.

12 ft

12 ft

$A =$ _____

Name _____ Date _____

You can find the areas of two more figures—trapezoids and circles—using formulas.

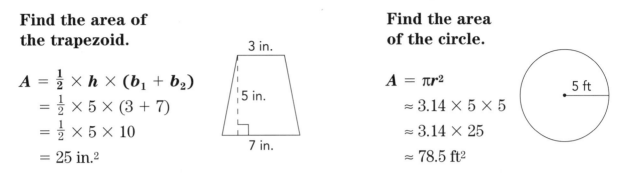

Find the area of the trapezoid.

$A = \frac{1}{2} \times h \times (b_1 + b_2)$
$= \frac{1}{2} \times 5 \times (3 + 7)$
$= \frac{1}{2} \times 5 \times 10$
$= 25$ in.²

3 in.
5 in.
7 in.

Find the area of the circle.

$A = \pi r^2$
$\approx 3.14 \times 5 \times 5$
$\approx 3.14 \times 25$
≈ 78.5 ft²

5 ft

Find the area of each trapezoid or circle. Use 3.14 for π.

304-305

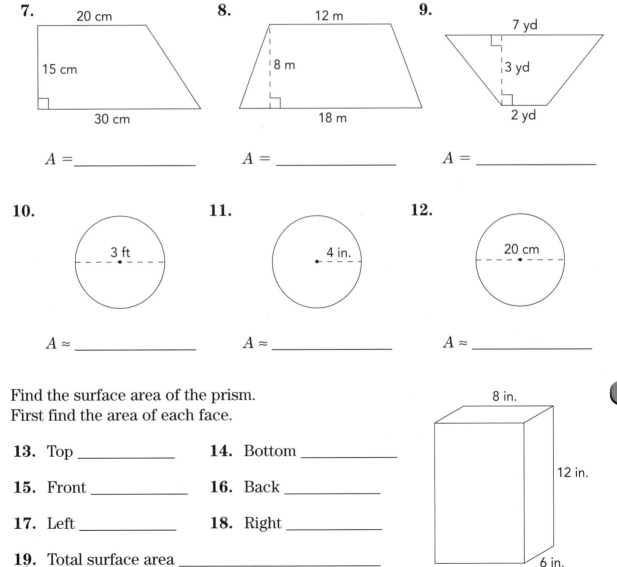

7.
20 cm
15 cm
30 cm

$A = $ _____

8.
12 m
8 m
18 m

$A = $ _____

9.
7 yd
3 yd
2 yd

$A = $ _____

10.
3 ft

$A \approx$ _____

11.
4 in.

$A \approx$ _____

12.
20 cm

$A \approx$ _____

Find the surface area of the prism. First find the area of each face.

307

8 in.
12 in.
6 in.

13. Top _____

14. Bottom _____

15. Front _____

16. Back _____

17. Left _____

18. Right _____

19. Total surface area _____

Name _____ Date _____

Area

Directions: Solve each problem. Mark your answer.

1. A rectangular parking lot is 80 feet long and 64 feet wide. What is the area of the lot?

   A. 288 ft²
   B. 500 ft²
   C. 2560 ft²
   D. 5120 ft²

2. Minnie made a jigsaw puzzle in the shape of a parallelogram. What is the area of the puzzle?

   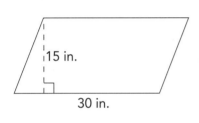

   A. 45 in.²
   B. 90 in.²
   C. 450 in.²
   D. 900 in.²

3. Stuart made a drawing of a triangular flag. What is the area of the flag?

   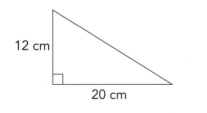

   A. 240 cm²
   B. 120 cm²
   C. 64 cm²
   D. 32 cm²

4. Find the area of this trapezoid.

   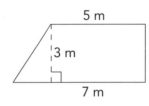

   A. 18 m²
   B. 21 m²
   C. 30 m²
   D. 36 m²

5. A circle has a radius of 8 mm. What is the area of the circle? (Use 3.14 for π.)

   A. 25.12 mm²
   B. 50.24 mm²
   C. 64 mm²
   D. 200.96 mm²

6. Ms. Casey bought a rectangular mobile home. What is the surface area of the 4 walls?

   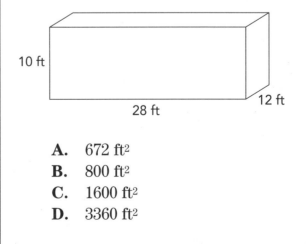

   A. 672 ft²
   B. 800 ft²
   C. 1600 ft²
   D. 3360 ft²

PRACTICE ANSWERS
Page 134
1. 85 km^2
2. 735 mm^2
3. 625 mi^2
4. $60\frac{3}{4}$ in.^{2}
5. 40.5 cm^2
6. 72 ft^2

Page 135
7. 375 cm^2
8. 120 m^2
9. 13.5 yd^2
10. 7.065 ft^2
11. 50.24 in.^{2}
12. 314 cm^2
13. 48 in.^{2}
14. 48 in.^{2}
15. 96 in.^{2}
16. 96 in.^{2}
17. 72 in.^{2}
18. 72 in.^{2}
19. 432 in.^{2}

TEST PREP ANSWERS
Page 136
1. D
2. C
3. B
4. A
5. D
6. B

Name _____ Date _____

Volume of Prisms

Find the volume of the rectangular prism.

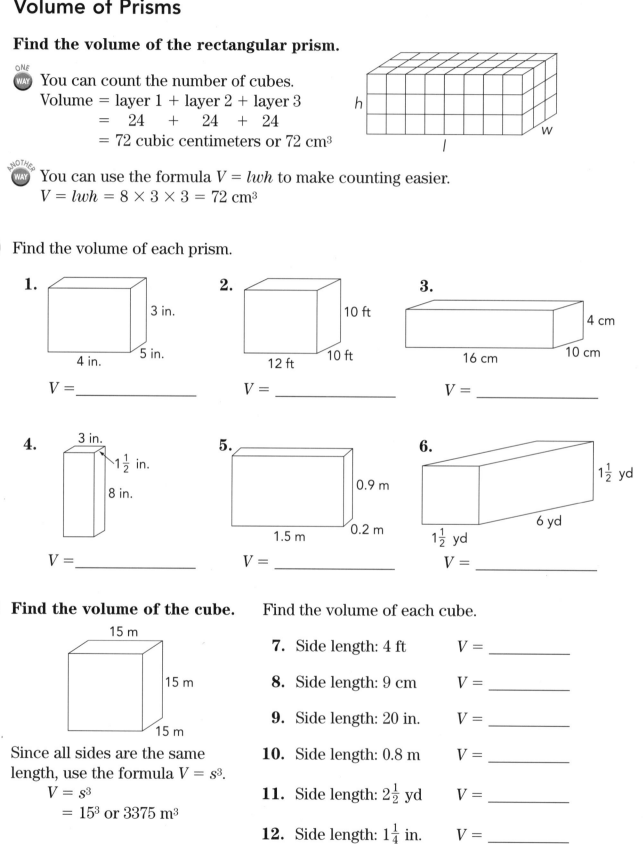

ONE WAY You can count the number of cubes.
Volume = layer 1 + layer 2 + layer 3
= 24 + 24 + 24
= 72 cubic centimeters or 72 cm³

ANOTHER WAY You can use the formula $V = lwh$ to make counting easier.
$V = lwh = 8 \times 3 \times 3 = 72$ cm³

---

310 Find the volume of each prism.

1.
3 in.
5 in.
4 in.

$V =$ _____

2.
10 ft
10 ft
12 ft

$V =$ _____

3.
4 cm
10 cm
16 cm

$V =$ _____

4.
3 in.
$1\frac{1}{2}$ in.
8 in.

$V =$ _____

5.
0.9 m
1.5 m
0.2 m

$V =$ _____

6.
$1\frac{1}{2}$ yd
6 yd
$1\frac{1}{2}$ yd

$V =$ _____

---

311 **Find the volume of the cube.**

15 m
15 m
15 m

Since all sides are the same length, use the formula $V = s^3$.
$V = s^3$
$= 15^3$ or 3375 m³

Find the volume of each cube.

7. Side length: 4 ft $V =$ _____

8. Side length: 9 cm $V =$ _____

9. Side length: 20 in. $V =$ _____

10. Side length: 0.8 m $V =$ _____

11. Side length: $2\frac{1}{2}$ yd $V =$ _____

12. Side length: $1\frac{1}{4}$ in. $V =$ _____

Name _____ Date _____

Volume of Prisms

Directions: Choose the best answer to each question. Mark your answer.

1 Carol made this figure with cubes. What is the volume of this figure?

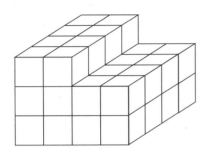

  A. 48 cubic units
  B. 40 cubic units
  C. 36 cubic units
  D. 32 cubic units

2 Velma got a new suitcase. What is the volume of the suitcase?

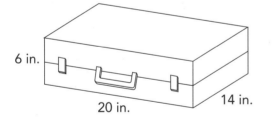

6 in.   20 in.   14 in.

  A. 84 in.³
  B. 120 in.³
  C. 280 in.³
  D. 1680 in.³

3 What is the volume of a cube that is 4 cm wide?

  A. 64 cm³
  B. 48 cm³
  C. 16 cm³
  D. 12 cm³

4 Sean used 1-inch cubes to make a building 8 inches long, 4 inches wide, and 2 inches high. If he uses the same cubes to make a building that is 4 inches long and 2 inches wide, how high will the new building be?

  A. 4 in.
  B. 6 in.
  C. 8 in.
  D. 16 in.

5 What is the volume of the truck shown below?

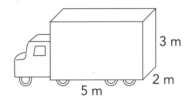

3 m   2 m   5 m

  A. 10 m³
  B. 15 m³
  C. 25 m³
  D. 30 m³

6 Mr. Ross built a storage bin for firewood. What is the volume of the bin?

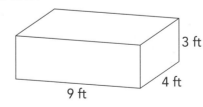

3 ft   4 ft   9 ft

  A. 108 ft³
  B. 63 ft³
  C. 36 ft³
  D. 21 ft³

PRACTICE ANSWERS
Page 138

1. 60 in.^{3}
2. 1200 ft^3
3. 640 cm^3
4. 36 in.^{3}
5. 0.27 m^3
6. $13\frac{1}{2}$ yd^3
7. 64 ft^3
8. 729 cm^3
9. 8000 in.^{3}
10. 0.512 m^3
11. $15\frac{5}{8}$ yd^3
12. $1\frac{61}{64}$ in.^{3}

TEST PREP ANSWERS
Page 139

1. B
2. D
3. A
4. C
5. D
6. A

Name _____　　Date _____

Capacity

How can you decide how much paint you need for a particular job? Use what you know about units of capacity.

How much paint might you need to paint a whole house—8 gallons or 1 pint?

Think: It takes a lot of paint—at least as much as a few milk cartons—to cover a whole house. Choose the larger amount, 8 gallons.

How much paint might you need to paint the front door of a house—1 milliliter or 0.5 liter?

Think: 1 milliliter is the amount in 1 cubic centimeter. It is less than a teaspoon. Choose the larger amount, 0.5 liter.

Circle the more reasonable measure of the capacity of each item.

313-315

1. A wash tub: 10 pints or 10 gallons

2. A bottle of fingernail polish: 5 milliliters or 5 liters

3. A car's gas tank: 10 quarts or 10 gallons

4. A container for a single serving of yogurt: 1 cup or 1 quart

5. A kitchen sink: 3 pints or 6 gallons

6. A bottle of shoe polish: 25 milliliters or 25 liters

7. A washing machine: 15 quarts or 15 gallons

8. A lunch-box thermos bottle: $1\frac{1}{2}$ cups or $1\frac{1}{2}$ quarts

9. A child's wading pool: 40 pints or 40 gallons

10. A picnic jug: 3 cups or 3 quarts

11. An ice cube tray: 500 milliliters or 5 liters

12. A sugar bowl: 25 milliliters or 0.25 liters

Name _____   Date _____

Capacity

Directions: Choose the best answer to each question. Mark your answer.

1 $1\frac{1}{2}$ cups is equal to how many ounces?

   (A)   6 oz

   (B)   8 oz

   (C)   12 oz

   (D)   24 oz

2   4 gallons is equal to how many quarts?

   (F)   128 qt

   (G)   64 qt

   (H)   32 qt

   (I)   16 qt

3   How many cups can you fill from a pint of milk?

   (A)   2

   (B)   4

   (C)   6

   (D)   8

4   The Pierces bought a wading pool for two small children. Which is the most likely measure of water needed to fill the pool?

   (F)   50 cups

   (G)   50 pints

   (H)   50 gallons

   (I)   50 quarts

5 $2\frac{1}{2}$ quarts is equal to how many ounces?

   (A)   120 oz

   (B)   80 oz

   (C)   60 oz

   (D)   40 oz

6   Andrew bought a 1-liter bottle of water. About how many cups of water did he buy?

   (F)   2

   (G)   4

   (H)   8

   (I)   16

7   Which of these could be served in one teaspoon?

   (A)   10 oz of juice

   (B)   10 L of water

   (C)   10 pt of maple syrup

   (D)   10 mL of medicine

8   About how many liters of gasoline would it take to fill a 10-gallon tank?

   (F)   4 L

   (G)   40 L

   (H)   400 L

   (I)   4000 L

PRACTICE ANSWERS
Page 141

1. 10 gallons
2. 5 milliliters
3. 10 gallons
4. 1 cup
5. 6 gallons
6. 25 milliliters
7. 15 gallons
8. $1\frac{1}{2}$ cups
9. 40 gallons
10. 3 quarts
11. 500 milliliters
12. 0.25 liters

TEST PREP ANSWERS
Page 142

1. C
2. I
3. A
4. H
5. B
6. G
7. D
8. G

Name _____ Date _____

Weight and Mass

How can you decide about how much an object weighs?
Use what you know about units of weight and mass.

Which is the more likely weight of a
dinner plate—20 ounces or 20 pounds?

Think: A dinner plate is not as heavy as 20
boxes of butter or margarine. Choose 20 ounces.

Which is the more likely weight of a
gallon of milk— 4 grams or 4 kilograms?

Think: A gallon of milk is similar in
weight to 4 textbooks. Choose 4 kilograms.

316-318 Circle the more reasonable measure of the weight or mass of each object.

1. A sneaker: 1 ounce or 1 pound

2. An empty wallet: 8 ounces or 8 pounds

3. A soup spoon: 25 grams or 25 kilograms

4. A greeting card: 2 ounces or 2 pounds

5. A full dump truck: 50 pounds or 5 tons

6. An adult: 80 grams or 80 kilograms

7. A Sunday newspaper: 5 pounds or 0.5 ton

8. An elephant: 500 pounds or 5 tons

9. A walk-behind lawn mower: 50 pounds or 1 ton

10. A ring for your finger: 4 grams or 0.4 kilograms

11. A mountain bike: 25 ounces or 25 pounds

12. An airplane: 500 pounds or 50 tons

13. Which weighs more: a pound of feathers or a pound of iron? Explain.

_____

Name _____ Date _____

Weight and Mass

Directions: Choose the best answer to each question. Mark your answer.

1. $2\frac{1}{2}$ pounds is equal to how many ounces?

   A. 20 oz

   B. 30 oz

   C. 40 oz

   D. 50 oz

2. Which is most likely to weigh about 5 pounds?

   A. a carrot

   B. a strawberry

   C. a sandwich

   D. a watermelon

3. A pencil is most likely to weigh about —

   A. 1 ounce

   B. 1 pound

   C. 10 ounces

   D. 10 pounds

4. $\frac{3}{4}$ ton is equal to how many pounds?

   A. 1000 lb

   B. 1500 lb

   C. 2000 lb

   D. 2500 lb

5. What is the most likely mass of a bag of 10 to 12 apples?

   A. 20 g

   B. 2 g

   C. 20 kg

   D. 2 kg

6. $\frac{1}{2}$ kg is equal to —

   A. 5 g

   B. 50 g

   C. 500 g

   D. 5000 g

7. Which is most likely to have a mass of about 5 grams?

   A. a spoonful of sugar

   B. a brick

   C. a loaf of bread

   D. a basketball

8. A man who is six feet tall is most likely to have a mass of —

   A. 80 oz

   B. 80 kg

   C. 80 lb

   D. 80 g

PRACTICE ANSWERS
Page 144

1. 1 pound
2. 8 ounces
3. 25 grams
4. 2 ounces
5. 5 tons
6. 80 kilograms
7. 5 pounds
8. 5 tons
9. 50 pounds
10. 4 grams
11. 25 pounds
12. 50 tons
13. They both weigh one pound, but a pound of feathers would take up much more space.

TEST PREP ANSWERS
Page 145

1. C
2. D
3. A
4. B
5. D
6. C
7. A
8. B

Name _____ Date _____

Temperature

Degrees Fahrenheit and degrees Celsius are
both used to measure temperature.

Water freezes at	32°F	0°C
Water boils at	212°F	100°C
Room temperature is about	70°F	20°C

Water at 50°F is like very cool tap water.
Water at 50°C is scalding hot, similar to water
in a dishwasher.

Circle the more reasonable temperature for each situation.

319-321

1. Water in an outdoor pool in summer: 80°F or 80°C

2. Lemonade from the refrigerator: 5°F or 5°C

3. A hot day at the beach: 35°F or 35°C

4. A snowy afternoon: 20°F or 20°C

5. A spring morning: 60°F or 60°C

6. Interior of a home freezer: 2°F or 2°C

Use the thermometer at the top of the page. Circle the best estimate
of an equivalent temperature for each temperature given.

7. 10°C is about	40°F	50°F	60°F
8. 30°C is between	30°–40°F	50°–60°F	80°–90°F
9. ⁻10°C is between	⁻10°–0°F	0°–10°F	10°–20°F
10. 50°C is between	120°–130°F	150°–160°F	190°–200°F
11. ⁻40°C is exactly	⁻20°F	⁻40°F	⁻10°F
12. 10°F is between	0°–⁻10°C	⁻10°–⁻20°C	⁻20°–⁻30°C
13. 40°F is about	5°C	10°C	20°C
14. 100°F is between	10°–20°C	20°–30°C	30°–40°C

Name _____   Date _____

Temperature

Directions: Read the thermometers. Write the temperature in both Fahrenheit and Celsius.

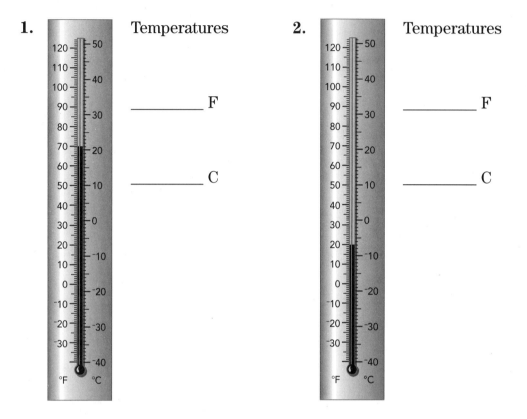

1.   Temperatures

_____ F

_____ C

2.   Temperatures

_____ F

_____ C

3. In the United States in July, the temperature is most likely to be about —

   A   80°F

   B   55°F

   C   40°F

   D   10°F

4. In Canada in December, the temperature is most likely to be about —

   E   30°C

   F   20°C

   G   10°C

   H   ⁻5°C

PRACTICE ANSWERS
Page 147

1. 80°F
2. 5°C
3. 35°C
4. 20°F
5. 60°F
6. 2°F
7. 50°F
8. 80°–90°F
9. 10°–20°F
10. 120°–130°F
11. ⁻40°F
12. ⁻10°–⁻20°C
13. 5°C
14. 30°–40°C

TEST PREP ANSWERS
Page 148

1. 70°F
   21°C
2. 20°F
   ⁻7°C
3. A
4. H

Name _____ Date _____

Time

Time Zones of Some U.S. Cities			
Eastern	**Central**	**Mountain**	**Pacific**
Baltimore	Chicago	Denver	Seattle
Orlando	Dallas	Phoenix	Los Angeles
New York	St. Louis	Boise	Las Vegas

Travel time between cities in the same time zone is just the difference between the arrival and departure times. If the cities are in different time zones, you must adjust one of the times for the time difference.

If you leave St. Louis at 9:25 A.M. and arrive at Chicago at 1:00 P.M., what is the travel time?

Think: The cities are in the same time zone. So, from 9:25 to 12:25 is 3 hours. From 12:25 to 1:00 P.M. is 35 minutes. The elapsed time is 3 hours 35 minutes.

If you leave Orlando at 10:05 A.M. and arrive in Denver at 12:30 P.M., what is the travel time?

ONE WAY **Think**: When I arrived in Denver, it was 2 hours later in Orlando. Using Orlando time, I traveled from 10:05 A.M. to 2:30 P.M., or 4 hours 25 minutes.

ANOTHER WAY Use Denver time instead. **Think**: I traveled from 8:05 A.M. to 12:30 P.M. Denver time. This is also 4 hours 25 minutes.

224-225 Find the elapsed time for each trip.

1. Leave Las Vegas: 8:15 A.M.; Arrive Seattle: 12:35 P.M. _____

2. Leave Dallas: 1:25 P.M.; Arrive Chicago: 3:50 P.M. _____

3. Leave New York: 6:40 A.M.; Arrive Orlando: 10:15 A.M. _____

4. Leave Boise: 8:15 A.M.; Arrive Phoenix: 2:05 P.M. _____

5. Leave Los Angles: 3:15 P.M.; Arrive New York: 12:35 A.M. _____

6. Leave Chicago: 7:20 A.M.; Arrive Denver: 9:15 A.M. _____

7. Leave Baltimore: 2:35 P.M.; Arrive Boise: 8:20 P.M. _____

8. Leave Phoenix: 3:55 P.M.; Arrive: Baltimore: 11:20 P.M. _____

Name _____   Date _____

Time

Directions: Choose the best answer to each question. Mark your answer.

1. A movie begins at 4:45 P.M. and lasts 1 hour 30 minutes. What time will the movie end?

   ○ **A.** 5:45 P.M.

   ○ **B.** 6:00 P.M.

   ○ **C.** 6:15 P.M.

2. Joe's soccer game started at 11:00 A.M. and ended at 12:15 P.M. How long did the game last?

   ○ **A.** 2 hr, 15 min

   ○ **B.** 1 hr, 15 min

   ○ **C.** 45 min

3. A train leaves New York City at 1:25 P.M. and arrives in Boston at 5:10 P.M. How long does the trip take?

   ○ **A.** 3 hr, 45 min

   ○ **B.** 3 hr, 35 min

   ○ **C.** 3 hr, 15 min

4. Sherry is making a schedule of her activities. Her dance class starts at 9:15 A.M. on Saturday and lasts 1 hour and 15 minutes. What time will the class end?

   ○ **A.** 10:15 A.M.

   ○ **B.** 10:30 A.M.

   ○ **C.** 11:00 A.M.

Use the time zone map below to answer questions 5–6.

5. If it is 10:00 A.M. in Los Angeles, what time is it in Atlanta?

   ○ **A.** 7:00 A.M.

   ○ **B.** 12:00 NOON

   ○ **C.** 1:00 P.M.

6. A plane leaves Cleveland at 4:30 P.M. and flies to Phoenix. The flight takes 3 hours. What time is it in Phoenix when the plane arrives?

   ○ **A.** 5:30 P.M.

   ○ **B.** 6:30 P.M.

   ○ **C.** 7:30 P.M.

PRACTICE ANSWERS
Page 150
1. 4 hours 20 minutes
2. 2 hours 25 minutes
3. 3 hours 35 minutes
4. 5 hours 50 minutes
5. 6 hours 20 minutes
6. 2 hours 55 minutes
7. 7 hours 45 minutes
8. 5 hours 25 minutes

TEST PREP ANSWERS
Page 151
1. C
2. B
3. A
4. B
5. C
6. A

Name _____ Date _____

Computing with Measures

You can use equivalent measures to help you change from one unit of measure to another.

Write 234 inches as yards.

Think: There are not very many yards in this distance, since yards are so much larger than inches. So divide by 36.
$234 \div 36 = 6\frac{1}{2}$ yards

Write 25 millimeters as centimeters.

Think: Centimeters are larger than millimeters, so it will take fewer of them to equal the same length. Divide by 10.
$25 \div 10 = 2.5$ centimeters

EQUIVALENT MEASURES
Customary Units of Length
1 foot (ft) = 12 inches (in.)
1 yard (yd) = 3 feet (36 inches)
1 mile (mi) = 1760 yards (5280 feet)
Metric Units of Length
1 centimeter (cm) = 10 millimeters (mm)
1 meter (m) = 100 centimeters
1 kilometer (km) = 1000 meters
Customary Units of Capacity
1 cup (c) = 8 ounces (oz)
1 pint (pt) = 2 cups
1 quart (qt) = 2 pints (4 cups)
1 gallon (gal) = 4 quarts (8 pints)

Write an equivalent measure for each given measure. Show your work.

327

1. 108 in. = _____ ft

2. 3 mi = _____ yd

3. 96 in. = _____ yd

4. 10,560 ft = _____ mi

5. 129 in. = _____ ft

6. 32 qt = _____ gal

7. 3 c = _____ oz

8. $3\frac{1}{2}$ qt = _____ pt

9. 25 pt = _____ qt

10. 36 oz = _____ c

11. 3.6 cm = _____ mm

12. 460 cm = _____ m

13. 0.5 km = _____ m

14. 108 mm = _____ cm

Name _____ Date _____

When you add and subtract mixed measures, be sure you regroup correctly.

Add: 3 gal 3 qt + 6 gal 2 qt

ONE WAY Add as mixed measures. Then regroup.

$$3 \text{ gal } 3 \text{ qt}$$
$$\underline{+\ 6 \text{ gal } 2 \text{ qt}}$$
$$9 \text{ gal } 5 \text{ qt} = 10 \text{ gal } 1 \text{ qt}$$

ANOTHER WAY Add as all quarts. Then regroup.

$$3 \text{ gal } 3 \text{ qt} = \quad 15 \text{ qt}$$
$$6 \text{ gal } 2 \text{ qt} = \underline{+\ 26 \text{ qt}}$$
$$41 \text{ qt}$$

$$41 \text{ qt} = 10 \text{ gal } 1 \text{ qt}$$

ANOTHER WAY Add as all gallons. Then regroup.

$$3 \text{ gal } 3 \text{ qt} = \quad 3\tfrac{3}{4} \text{ gal}$$
$$6 \text{ gal } 2 \text{ qt} = \underline{+6\tfrac{2}{4} \text{ gal}}$$
$$9\tfrac{5}{4} \text{ gal}$$

$$9\tfrac{5}{4} \text{ gal} = 10 \text{ gal } 1 \text{ qt}$$

328-330 Add or subtract. Show your work.

15. 6 yd 2 ft + 3 yd 2 ft = _____

16. 9 ft 8 in. + 7 ft 5 in. = _____

17. 9 qt − 3 qt 1 pt = _____

18. 5 ft 7 in. − 3 ft 10 in. = _____

19. 3 c 6 oz + 2 c 5 oz = _____

20. 4 yd 16 in. + 5 yd 20 in. = _____

21. 6 gal 1 qt − 4 gal 3 qt = _____

22. 8 yd 1 ft − 3 yd 2 ft = _____

23. 9 ft 9 in. + 7 ft 11 in. = _____

24. 1 mi 1100 ft + 2 mi 4400 ft = _____

25. 5 gal 3 pt − 3 gal 7 pt = _____

26. 12 qt 1 c − 9 qt 2 c = _____

27. 4 yd 10 in. + 6 yd 25 in. = _____

28. 3 gal 2 qt + 6 gal 2 qt = _____

Name _____ Date _____

You can multiply and divide mixed measures either by a number or by another measure. Be sure to use the correct labels on your answers.

A roll of crepe paper is 9 ft 8 in. long.
How long can you make 4 streamers of equal length?

ONE WAY You can regroup as you divide.

$$
\begin{array}{r}
2\text{ ft }5\text{ in.} \\
4\overline{)9\text{ ft }8\text{ in.}} \\
-8\text{ ft} \\
\hline
1\text{ ft }8\text{ in.} = 20\text{ in.} \\
-20\text{ in.} \\
\hline
0
\end{array}
$$

ANOTHER WAY You can regroup first using inches.

9 ft 8 in. = 108 + 8 = 116 in.

Then,

116 in. ÷ 4 = 29 in.

= 2 ft 5 in.

ANOTHER WAY You can regroup first using feet.

9 ft 8 in. = $9\frac{8}{12}$ or $9\frac{2}{3}$ ft

$9\frac{2}{3} \div 4 = \frac{29}{3} \times \frac{1}{4}$

$= \frac{29}{12}$ or $2\frac{5}{12}$ ft

= 2 ft 5 in.

The sides of a rectangle are 3 ft 2 in. and 1 ft 3 in. long.
What is the area of the rectangle?

ONE WAY You can write both lengths in inches. Then multiply.

3 ft 2 in. = 38 in.   1 ft 3 in. = 15 in.

$A = 38 \times 15$

$= 570$ in.^{2}

ANOTHER WAY You can write both lengths in feet. Then multiply.

3 ft 2 in. = $3\frac{1}{6}$ ft   1 ft 3 in. = $1\frac{1}{4}$ ft

$A = 3\frac{1}{6} \times 1\frac{1}{4} = \frac{19}{6} \times \frac{5}{4}$

$= \frac{95}{24}$ or $3\frac{23}{24}$ ft^2

Multiply or divide. Show your work.

331-332

29. 9 ft 2 in. × 6 = _____

30. 8 gal 3 qt ÷ 5 = _____

31. 3 c 5 oz × 4 = _____

32. 1 lb 4 oz ÷ 5 oz = _____

33. 2 ft 6 in. × 9 ft = _____

34. 4 lb 11 oz ÷ 1 lb 9 oz = _____

Name _____   Date _____

Computing with Measures

Directions: Choose the best answer to each question. Mark your answer.

1 A garden wall is 17 feet long. How many yards long is the wall?

- **A** $4\frac{1}{3}$ yd
- **B** $4\frac{2}{3}$ yd
- **C** $5\frac{1}{3}$ yd
- **D** $5\frac{2}{3}$ yd

2 Max found a snake that was $2\frac{1}{2}$ feet long. What is the length of the snake in inches?

- **F** 15 in.
- **G** 25 in.
- **H** 30 in.
- **J** 36 in.

3 Colleen made $4\frac{1}{2}$ gallons of lemonade. How many quarts did she make?

- **A** 26 qt
- **B** 18 qt
- **C** 13 qt
- **D** 9 qt

4 A ski trail is 1850 meters long. What is the length in kilometers?

- **F** 1.85 km
- **G** 18.5 km
- **H** 185 km
- **J** 18,500 km

5 In 2 jumps, Calvin jumped 3 ft 8 in. and 4 ft 6 in. How far did he jump all together?

- **A** 6 ft 4 in.
- **B** 7 ft 2 in.
- **C** 7 ft 4 in.
- **D** 8 ft 2 in.

6 Rick's car is 14 ft 7 in. long. John's pickup truck is 22 ft 3 in. long. How much longer is John's truck?

- **F** 7 ft 5 in.
- **G** 7 ft 8 in.
- **H** 8 ft 4 in.
- **J** 8 ft 10 in.

7 Claire installed 5 sections of split-rail fence. Each section is 8 ft 6 in. long. How long is the fence in all?

- **A** 34 ft
- **B** 40 ft 6 in.
- **C** 42 ft 6 in.
- **D** 70 ft

8 A farmer has 15 lb 12 oz of tomatoes. If she puts 1 lb 8 oz of tomatoes in each bag, how many bags can she fill?

- **F** 11 bags
- **G** $10\frac{1}{2}$ bags
- **H** 9 bags
- **J** $8\frac{1}{2}$ bags

PRACTICE ANSWERS
Page 153

1. 9 ft
2. 5280 yd
3. $2\frac{2}{3}$ yd
4. 2 mi
5. $10\frac{3}{4}$ ft
6. 8 gal
7. 24 oz
8. 7 pt
9. $12\frac{1}{2}$ qt
10. $4\frac{1}{2}$ c
11. 36 mm
12. 4.6 m
13. 500 m
14. 10.8 cm

Page 154

15. 10 yd 1 ft
16. 17 ft 1 in.
17. 5 qt 1 pt
18. 1 ft 9 in.
19. 6 c 3 oz
20. 10 yd
21. 1 gal 2 qt
22. 4 yd 2 ft
23. 17 ft 8 in.
24. 4 mi 220 ft
25. 1 gal 4 pt
26. 2 qt 3 c
27. 10 yd 35 in.
28. 10 gal

Page 155

29. 55 ft
30. 1 gal 3 qt
31. 14 c 4 oz
32. 4
33. $22\frac{1}{2}$ ft^2
34. 3

TEST PREP ANSWERS
Page 156

1. D
2. H
3. B
4. F
5. D
6. G
7. C
8. G

A Bird's-Eye View of Ravenslake

OBJECTIVES
- Determine the area of different polygons and irregular shapes
- Identify missing measures to calculate perimeter

MATERIALS
- Ravenslake Park Page, page 192
- calculators (optional)

TIME
- 45–60 minutes

TEACHER NOTES
- Students should be familiar with using formulas for calculating area and perimeter.

- Students may need help to understand how to use the grid method to find the approximate area of Ravenslake. Have a discussion about using this method before students do the activity.

- Discussion may be necessary for students to realize that the perimeter of the park can be used to find the length of the jogging path.

EXTENSIONS
- Students can trace the shapes of the special feature sections on grid paper and use the grid method to determine the areas.

- Another method of finding the area of an irregular shape is to divide it into smaller sections like rectangles or triangles and add the areas. Have the students make another approximation of the area of Ravenslake using this method.

- Design an outline of a park area that is made up of combinations of different geometric shapes. Have the students break the large area into smaller sections to determine the area of the park.

- Students can design a park of their own. Have them include special features like a petting zoo, a baseball diamond, a gazebo, and so on. They should assign shapes to these features and calculate the area of each one.

- Have the students investigate the dimensions of local tennis, basketball, or volleyball courts, baseball diamonds, and swimming pools. They can determine the area of each one.

ANSWERS
1. Trapezoid
2. $A = \frac{1}{2} \times h \times (b_1 + b_2)$
3. 900 ft^2
4. Circle
5. $A = \pi r^2$
6. 706.5 ft^2
7. Rectangle
8. $A = lw$
9. 1300 yd^2
10. Rectangle
11. $A = lw$
12. 2450 ft^2
13. Beginning at the top of the map and proceeding in a clockwise direction, the missing dimensions are 455 ft, 1365 ft, 910 ft, and 650 ft.
14. 1,079,487.5 ft^2
15. The area of the lake is approximately 270,400 ft^2.
16. Answers will vary. The perimeter of the park is 4227.5 ft, so a jogging path following the perimeter is easily one-half mile long.
17. Answers will vary. Hopefully, students will use the grids to help them calculate the approximate length.

Name _____ Date _____

A Bird's-Eye View of Ravenslake

The town of Ravenslake is creating a park for its residents. Within the park, there is space set aside for some special features. For each of these sections, write the name of the shape and the formula needed to determine its area. Then calculate the area of each section.

The jungle gym area

1. Shape: _____ 2. Formula: _____ 3. Area: _____

The merry-go-round (Use 3.14 for π.)

4. Shape: _____ 5. Formula: _____ 6. Area: _____

The parking lot

7. Shape: _____ 8. Formula: _____ 9. Area: _____

The volleyball court

10. Shape: _____ 11. Formula: _____ 12. Area: _____

13. On your Ravenslake Park Page, write the missing dimensions of the perimeter of the park.

14. What is the total area of the park? Use the back of this page for your calculations. _____

One way to find the area of an irregular shape is to use a grid as an overlay of the area. The Ravenslake Park Page already has a grid on it. Your job is to find the area of Ravenslake. First, estimate the area of the lake by counting the number of whole squares in its area. Then fill in partial squares to make whole squares.

15. Using this method, what is the approximate area of Ravenslake? _____

16. The park should include a jogging path that is at least one-half mile long. Sketch the location of the jogging path on your Ravenslake Park Page.

17. What is the approximate length of the jogging path you have sketched? _____

20 ft

30 ft

40 ft

Jungle Gym Area

30 ft

Merry-Go-Round

65 yd

20 yd

Parking Lot

70 yd

35 yd

Volleyball Court

Name _____ Date _____

Basic Ideas in Geometry

335-343   For each diagram, write the letter of its matching description.

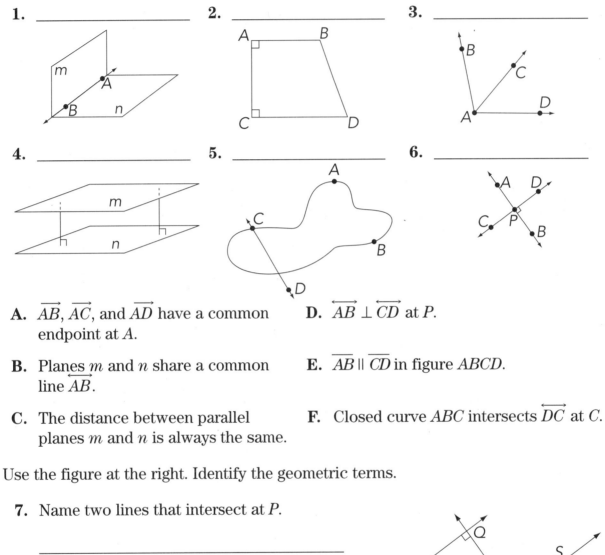

1. _____ 2. _____ 3. _____

4. _____ 5. _____ 6. _____

A. $\overrightarrow{AB}$, $\overrightarrow{AC}$, and $\overrightarrow{AD}$ have a common endpoint at A.

D. $\overleftrightarrow{AB} \perp \overleftrightarrow{CD}$ at P.

B. Planes m and n share a common line $\overleftrightarrow{AB}$.

E. $\overline{AB} \parallel \overline{CD}$ in figure $ABCD$.

C. The distance between parallel planes m and n is always the same.

F. Closed curve ABC intersects $\overleftrightarrow{DC}$ at C.

335-341   Use the figure at the right. Identify the geometric terms.

7. Name two lines that intersect at P.

_____

8. Name two pairs of perpendicular lines.

_____

9. Name two parallel lines.

_____

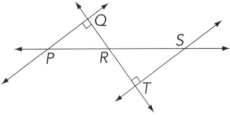

10. Name two rays that have R for an endpoint.

_____

Name _____ Date _____

Complete the crossword puzzle of geometric terms. Use the definitions below.

335-343

Across

1. A place in space
6. The number of points at which two parallel lines intersect
11. A part of a line that starts at *I* and goes on forever past *M*
12. A point is represented by a _____.
13. _____ lines form right angles.
14. A straight path that has no endpoints
15. To make a mistake
19. A part of a line with two endpoints
20. A flat surface that extends infinitely
21. The number of directions in which a line extends infinitely

Down

2. The number of points on a line
3. Parallel lines have ___ points in common.
4. Name of a segment whose endpoints are *T* and *N*
5. A smoothly bent line
7. $\overrightarrow{PQ}$ has its _____ point at *P*.
8. To meet or cross
9. A segment has two of these
10. Lines or planes that do not intersect
16. Angle formed by perpendicular lines
17. Number of points at which parallel planes intersect
18. Number of points at which two lines can intersect

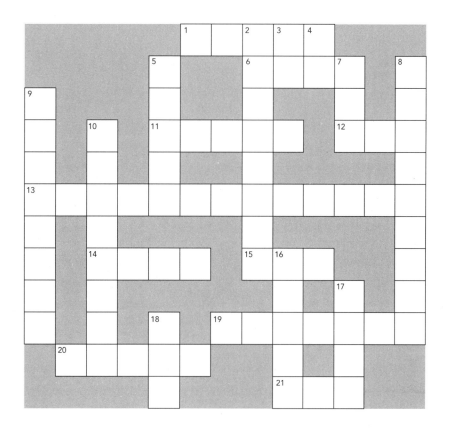

Name _____ Date _____

Basic Ideas in Geometry

Directions: Use the figure below to answer questions 1–5.

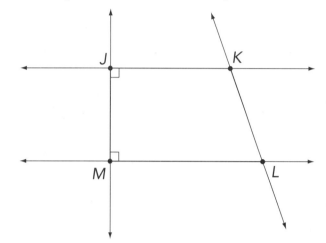

1.   Name a ray with endpoint *M*. _____

2.   Name two parallel lines. _____

3.   List four line segments. _____

4.   Name a line that is perpendicular to $\overleftrightarrow{JK}$. _____

5.   Name two lines that intersect. _____

6.   In the space below, draw an open curve and a closed curve.
   Label each curve.

PRACTICE ANSWERS
Page 160

1. B
2. E
3. A
4. C
5. F
6. D
7. $\overleftrightarrow{PS}$ and $\overleftrightarrow{PQ}$
8. $\overleftrightarrow{QT}$ and $\overleftrightarrow{ST}$; $\overleftrightarrow{PQ}$ and $\overleftrightarrow{QT}$
9. $\overleftrightarrow{PQ}$ and $\overleftrightarrow{TS}$
10. $\overrightarrow{RS}$, $\overrightarrow{RT}$, $\overrightarrow{RP}$, or $\overrightarrow{RQ}$

Page 161

					¹P	O	²I	³N	⁴T			⁸I

Crossword:

- ¹ P O I N T
- N O N ⁷E
- ⁵ C U F N ⁸ I N
- ⁹ E N D, ¹⁰ P, ¹¹ R A Y I M, ¹² D O T E
- D A V N T E
- ¹³ P E R P E N D I C U L A R S
- O A T E
- I ¹⁴ L I N E ¹⁵ E ¹⁶ R R C
- N L I ¹⁷ Z C
- T E ¹⁸ O ¹⁹ S E G M E N T
- ²⁰ P L A N E H R
- E ²¹ T W O

TEST PREP ANSWERS
Page 162

1. $\overrightarrow{MJ}$ or $\overrightarrow{ML}$
2. $\overleftrightarrow{JK}$ and $\overleftrightarrow{ML}$
3. $\overline{JM}$, $\overline{ML}$, $\overline{KL}$, and $\overline{JK}$
4. $\overrightarrow{JM}$
5. $\overleftrightarrow{JK}$ and $\overleftrightarrow{KL}$, $\overleftrightarrow{ML}$ and $\overleftrightarrow{KL}$, $\overleftrightarrow{JK}$ and $\overleftrightarrow{JM}$, or $\overleftrightarrow{JM}$ and $\overleftrightarrow{ML}$
6. Examples:

Open Curve

Closed Curve

Name _____ Date _____

Angles

346-347 Classify each angle as acute, right, obtuse, or straight. Use the diagram below.

1. ∠BQC _____

2. ∠BQD _____

3. ∠DQE _____

4. ∠CQE _____

5. ∠AQE _____

6. ∠AQB _____

349-353 Write the name of each angle or ray. Use the diagram below.

7. Name an angle bisector. _____

8. Name a pair of complementary angles.

_____

9. Name a pair of congruent angles.

_____

10. Name two rays that are perpendicular to each other.

_____

11. Name two adjacent angles.

_____

Write the names of the angles. Use the diagram at the right.

12. Name two supplementary angles.

_____

13. Name two vertical angles.

_____

14. Name two congruent angles.

_____

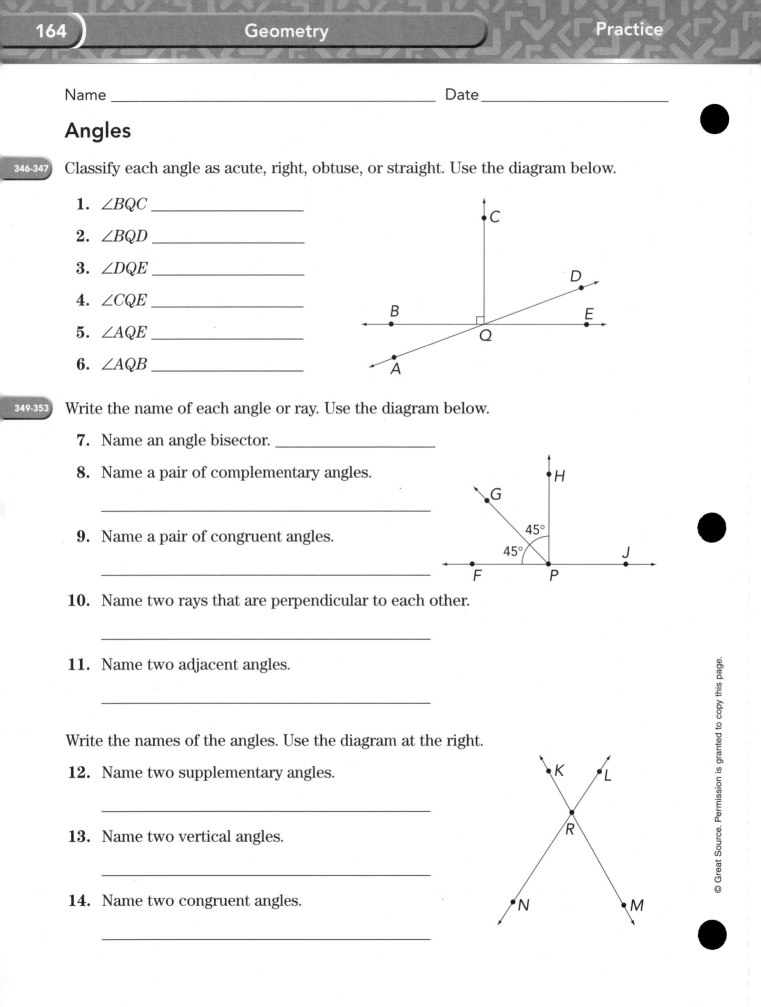

Name _____ Date _____

You can find the measure of an interior angle of a triangle
if you know the other two.
You can also find the measure of a central angle of a circle.

Find the measure of ∠B.

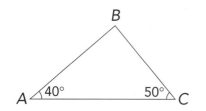

B

A 40°   50° C

Find the measure of ∠4.

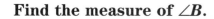

70°
∠4
40°

You know that ∠A + ∠B + ∠C = 180°,
and you also know the measures of
∠A and ∠C.

$$40° + ∠B + 50° = 180°$$
$$90° + ∠B = 180°$$
$$∠B = 90°$$

You know that ∠1 + ∠2 + ∠3 + ∠4 = 360°.
Substitute the measures you
already know.

$$70° + 90° + 40° + ∠4 = 360°$$
$$200° + ∠4 = 360°$$
$$∠4 = 160°$$

Find the measure of each angle.

`354-355`

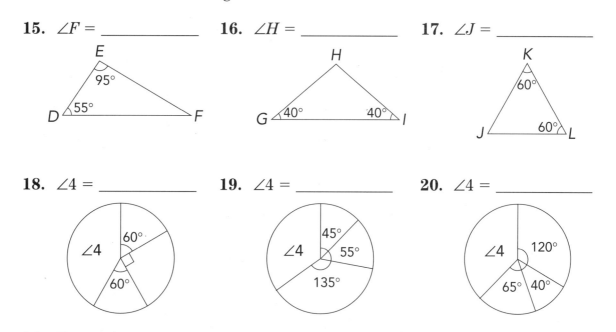

15. ∠F = _____

E
95°
55°
D   F

16. ∠H = _____

H
40°   40°
G   I

17. ∠J = _____

K
60°
J   60° L

18. ∠4 = _____

60°
∠4
60°

19. ∠4 = _____

45°
∠4   55°
135°

20. ∠4 = _____

∠4   120°
65° 40°

21. Two angles of a triangle are congruent. The other angle has a measure of 50°.

What is the measure of each of the congruent angles? _____

22. Five central angles of a circle are congruent.
What is the measure of each central angle? _____

Name _____   Date _____

Angles

Directions: Choose the best answer to each question. Mark your answer.

1. Meredith drew an angle measuring 60°. Which could be the angle that Meredith drew?

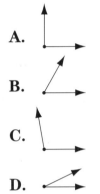

A.

B.

C.

D.

2. Which angle is obtuse?

A.

B.

C.

D.

3. What is the sum of angles *1*, *2*, and *3* in this triangle?

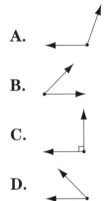

   A.   45°

   B.   90°

   C.   180°

   D.   360°

4. Figure *FGHJ* is a square. Which statement is true?

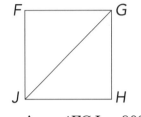

   A.   ∠*FGJ* = 90°

   B.   ∠*GJH* and ∠*GHJ* are supplementary.

   C.   ∠*JFG* = 45°

   D.   ∠*FJG* ≅ ∠*GJH*

Use the figure below to answer questions 5–6.

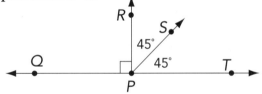

5. Which ray is an angle bisector?

   A. $\overrightarrow{PQ}$

   B. $\overrightarrow{PR}$

   C. $\overrightarrow{PS}$

   D. $\overrightarrow{PT}$

6. ∠*RPS* and ∠*SPT* are what kind of angles?

   A.   complementary

   B.   vertical

   C.   supplementary

   D.   straight

PRACTICE ANSWERS
Page 164

1. right
2. obtuse
3. acute
4. right
5. obtuse
6. acute
7. $\overrightarrow{PG}$
8. ∠*FPG* and ∠*GPH*
9. ∠*FPG* and ∠*GPH*, or ∠*FPH* and ∠*HPJ*
10. $\overrightarrow{PH}$ and $\overrightarrow{PJ}$, or $\overrightarrow{PH}$ and $\overrightarrow{PF}$
11. ∠*FPG* and ∠*GPH*, or ∠*GPH* and ∠*HPJ*
12. ∠*NRK* and ∠*KRL*, or ∠*KRL* and ∠*LRM*, or ∠*LRM* and ∠*MRN*, or ∠*MRN* and ∠*NRK*
13. ∠*LRM* and ∠*KRN*, or ∠*KRL* and ∠*NRM*
14. ∠*LRM* and ∠*KRN*, or ∠*KRL* and ∠*NRM*

Page 165

15. 30°
16. 100°
17. 60°
18. 150°
19. 125°
20. 135°
21. 65°
22. 72°

TEST PREP ANSWERS
Page 166

1. B
2. A
3. C
4. D
5. C
6. A

Name _____   Date _____

Plane Figures

You can classify a triangle by the size of its largest angle and
by the lengths of its sides.

Classify this triangle.

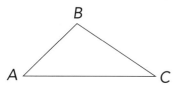

By angle size
The largest angle is ∠B, and it is greater than 90°.
The angle is obtuse and so is the triangle.

By side lengths
All of the sides have different lengths, so this
a scalene triangle.

361-363 Classify each triangle by angle size and by side lengths.

1.   **2.**   **3.**

angle: _____   angle: _____   angle: _____

sides: _____   sides: _____   sides: _____

Each side of a triangle is the shortest distance between its
two endpoints. So you can write three true inequalities
by looking at each side in turn.

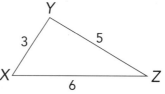

Look at side *XZ*. $6 < 3 + 5$
Look at side *XY*. $3 < 6 + 5$
Look at side *YZ*. $5 < 3 + 6$

360 Write three true inequalities for each triangle.

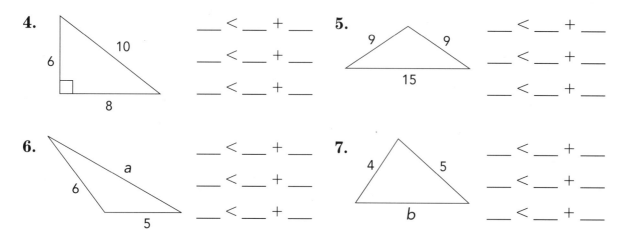

4.   ___ < ___ + ___   **5.**   ___ < ___ + ___
              ___ < ___ + ___   ___ < ___ + ___
              ___ < ___ + ___   ___ < ___ + ___

6.   ___ < ___ + ___   **7.**   ___ < ___ + ___
              ___ < ___ + ___   ___ < ___ + ___
              ___ < ___ + ___   ___ < ___ + ___

Name _____ Date _____

Quadrilaterals are polygons with four sides. There are five types of quadrilaterals.

Trapezoid	Parallelogram	Rhombus	Rectangle	Square
Exactly one pair of parallel sides	Opposite sides parallel and congruent	A parallelogram with four sides congruent	A parallelogram with four right angles	A rectangle with all four sides congruent

Circle all descriptions that apply to the figure. If none apply, draw an "X" through all the choices.

364-366

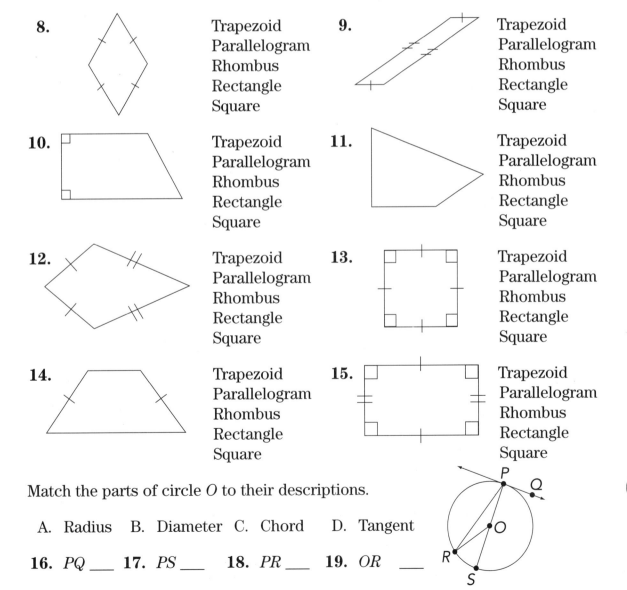

8. Trapezoid
   Parallelogram
   Rhombus
   Rectangle
   Square

9. Trapezoid
   Parallelogram
   Rhombus
   Rectangle
   Square

10. Trapezoid
    Parallelogram
    Rhombus
    Rectangle
    Square

11. Trapezoid
    Parallelogram
    Rhombus
    Rectangle
    Square

12. Trapezoid
    Parallelogram
    Rhombus
    Rectangle
    Square

13. Trapezoid
    Parallelogram
    Rhombus
    Rectangle
    Square

14. Trapezoid
    Parallelogram
    Rhombus
    Rectangle
    Square

15. Trapezoid
    Parallelogram
    Rhombus
    Rectangle
    Square

Match the parts of circle O to their descriptions.

367

A. Radius   B. Diameter   C. Chord   D. Tangent

16. PQ ___   17. PS ___   18. PR ___   19. OR ___

Name _____ Date _____

You can find the lengths of sides of similar triangles. First you need to know the ratio of one pair of corresponding sides.

$\triangle ABC \sim \triangle DEF$

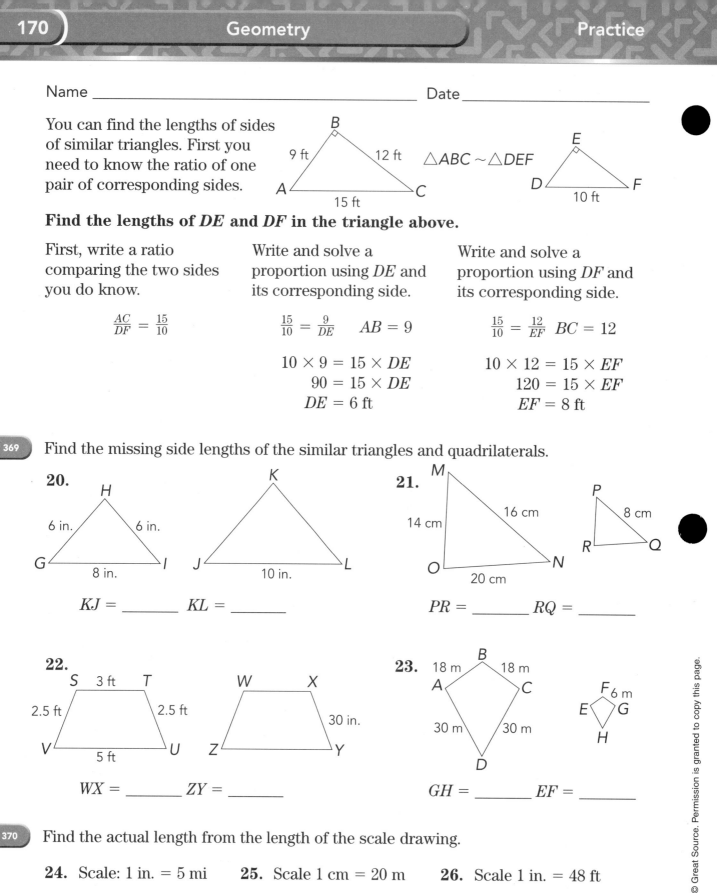

Find the lengths of *DE* and *DF* in the triangle above.

First, write a ratio comparing the two sides you do know.	Write and solve a proportion using *DE* and its corresponding side.	Write and solve a proportion using *DF* and its corresponding side.
$\frac{AC}{DF} = \frac{15}{10}$	$\frac{15}{10} = \frac{9}{DE}$ $AB = 9$	$\frac{15}{10} = \frac{12}{EF}$ $BC = 12$
	$10 \times 9 = 15 \times DE$	$10 \times 12 = 15 \times EF$
	$90 = 15 \times DE$	$120 = 15 \times EF$
	$DE = 6$ ft	$EF = 8$ ft

369 Find the missing side lengths of the similar triangles and quadrilaterals.

20.

$KJ =$ _____ $KL =$ _____

21.

$PR =$ _____ $RQ =$ _____

22.

$WX =$ _____ $ZY =$ _____

23.

$GH =$ _____ $EF =$ _____

370 Find the actual length from the length of the scale drawing.

24. Scale: 1 in. = 5 mi

Scale length: $3\frac{1}{2}$ in.

Actual length: _____

25. Scale 1 cm = 20 m

Scale length: 2.8 cm

Actual length: _____

26. Scale 1 in. = 48 ft

Scale length: $4\frac{7}{8}$ in.

Actual length: _____

Name _____ Date _____

There are three transformations that will form congruent figures.

Translation or slide	**Reflection or flip**	**Rotation or turn**

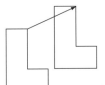 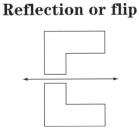 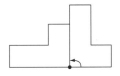

Every point moves the same distance and direction to form a new figure. It can be represented by a slide arrow.

Every point moves to the opposite side of a line, called the line of reflection, to form a new figure.

Every point rotates a given angle and direction about a center point, called the turn center, to form a new figure.

Write whether a translation, reflection or rotation is shown. Then draw the translation arrow, the line of reflection, or the turn center.

375-379

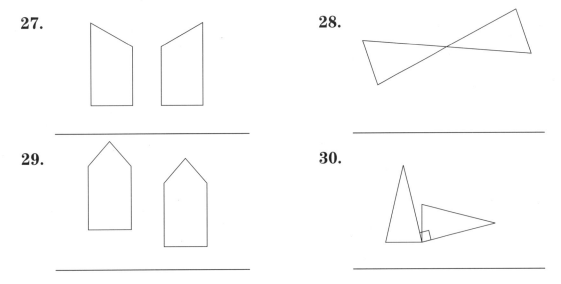

27. _____

28. _____

29. _____

30. _____

Write whether each set of 5 squares (called pentominoes) shows *line* symmetry, *turn* symmetry, *both*, or *neither*. Draw the line of symmetry or the turn center.

378, 380

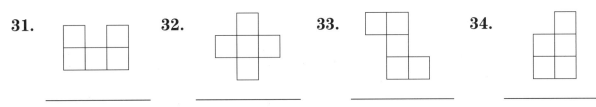

31. _____

32. _____

33. _____

34. _____

35. Which of the pentominoes in questions 31–34 can be used to tessellate a plane? _____

381

Name _____ Date _____

Plane Figures

Directions: Choose the best answer to each question. Mark your answer.

1 Look at the group of figures.

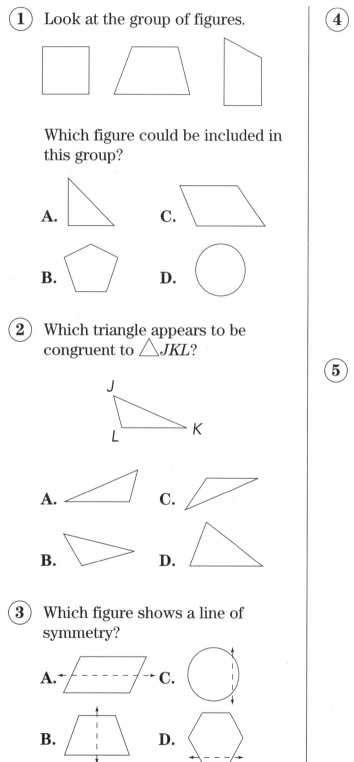

Which figure could be included in this group?

A.

C.

B.

D.

2 Which triangle appears to be congruent to △*JKL*?

A.

C.

B.

D.

3 Which figure shows a line of symmetry?

A.

C.

B.

D.

4 Jenna made a scale drawing of her rectangular room. What is the area of the room?

Scale: 1 in. = 6 ft

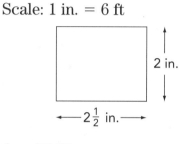

2 in.

$2\frac{1}{2}$ in.

A. 27 ft²

B. 54 ft²

C. 90 ft²

D. 180 ft²

5 Which picture shows a reflection of the flag?

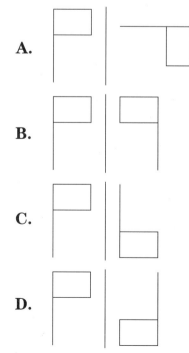

A.

B.

C.

D.

PRACTICE ANSWERS
Page 168

1. Acute, isosceles
2. Acute, equilateral
3. Right, scalene
4. $6 < 8 + 10$; $8 < 6 + 10$; $10 < 6 + 8$
5. $9 < 9 + 15$; $9 < 9 + 15$; $15 < 9 + 9$
6. $6 < a + 5$; $5 < a + 6$; $a < 6 + 5$
7. $5 < 4 + b$; $4 < 5 + b$; $b < 4 + 5$

Page 169

8. Parallelogram, rhombus
9. Parallelogram
10. Trapezoid
11. None apply.
12. None apply.
13. Parallelogram, rhombus, rectangle, square
14. Trapezoid
15. Parallelogram, rectangle
16. D
17. B
18. C
19. A

Page 170

20. $KJ = 7\frac{1}{2}$ in.; $KL = 7\frac{1}{2}$ in.
21. $PR = 7$ cm; $RQ = 10$ cm
22. $WX = 36$ in.; $ZY = 60$ in.
23. $GH = 10$ m; $EF = 6$ m
24. $17\frac{1}{2}$ mi
25. 56 m
26. 234 ft

Page 171

27. Reflection
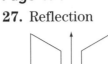

28. Rotation

29. Translation

30. Rotation
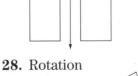

31. Line symmetry

32. Both line and turn symmetry

33. Turn symmetry

34. Neither
35. The ones in questions 32, 33, and 34

TEST PREP ANSWERS
Page 172

1. C
2. A
3. B
4. D
5. B

Name _____ Date _____

Solid Figures

383-387 For each shape, write the letter of its name and the letter of its net.

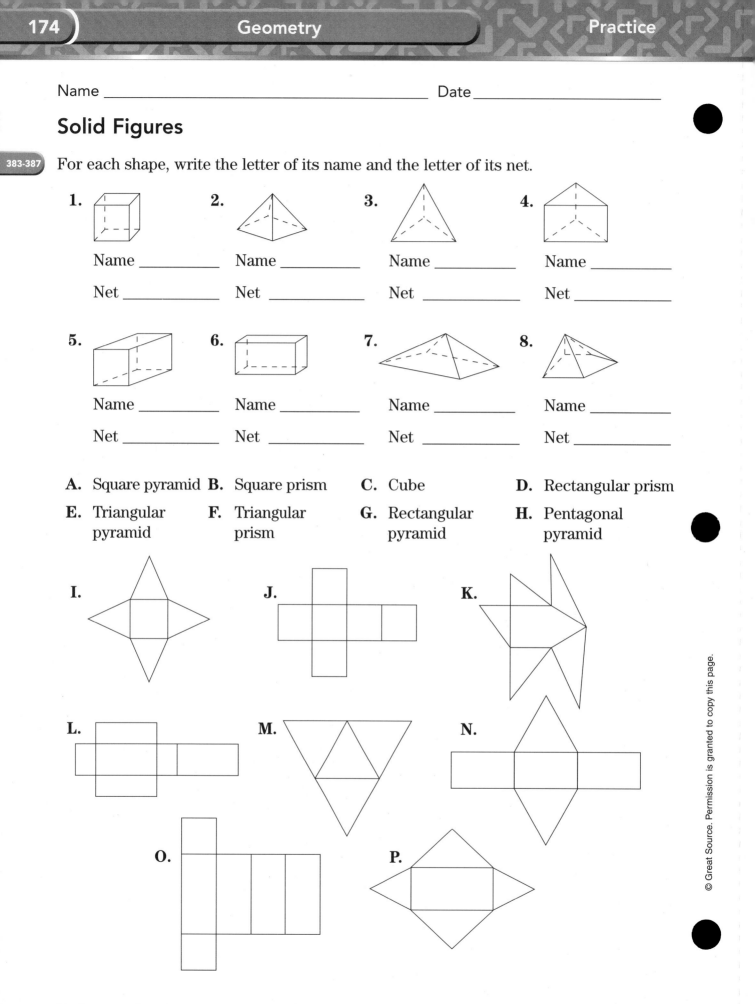

1.

Name _____

Net _____

2.

Name _____

Net _____

3.

Name _____

Net _____

4.

Name _____

Net _____

5.

Name _____

Net _____

6.

Name _____

Net _____

7.

Name _____

Net _____

8.

Name _____

Net _____

A. Square pyramid **B.** Square prism **C.** Cube **D.** Rectangular prism

E. Triangular pyramid **F.** Triangular prism **G.** Rectangular pyramid **H.** Pentagonal pyramid

I.

J.

K.

L.

M.

N.

O.

P.

Name _____ Date _____

Identify whether each net is for a prism, pyramid, cylinder or cone.

`384-391`

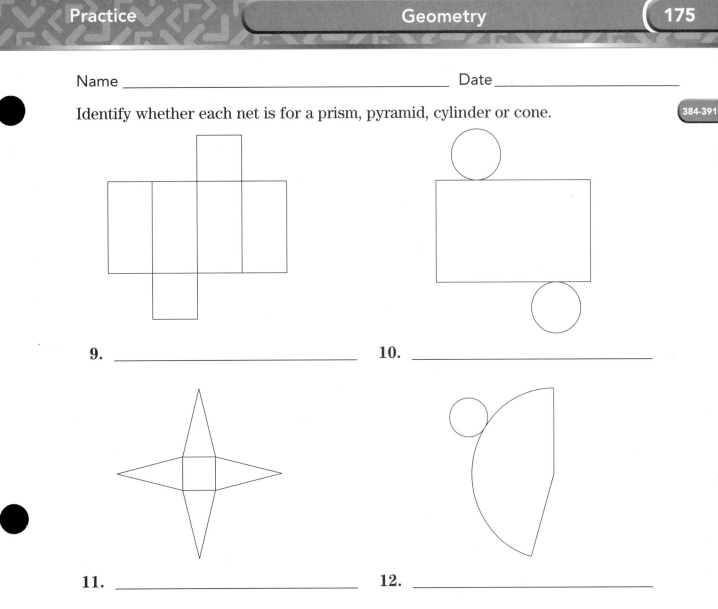

9. _____

10. _____

11. _____

12. _____

On the grid below, draw the figures that would result from folding the nets above. Use items 475–478 of the Almanac in *Math at Hand* to help you.

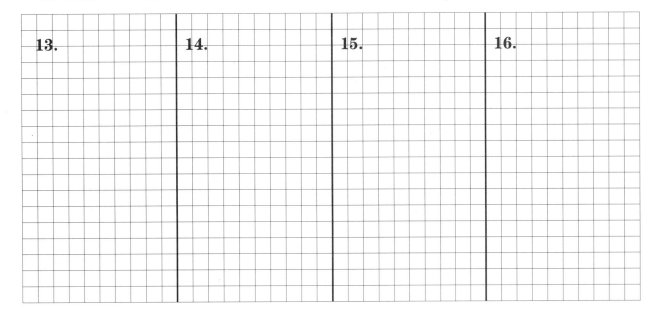

13.

14.

15.

16.

Name _____ Date _____

Solid Figures

Directions: Write the name of each figure on the line.
Then draw a net of each figure.

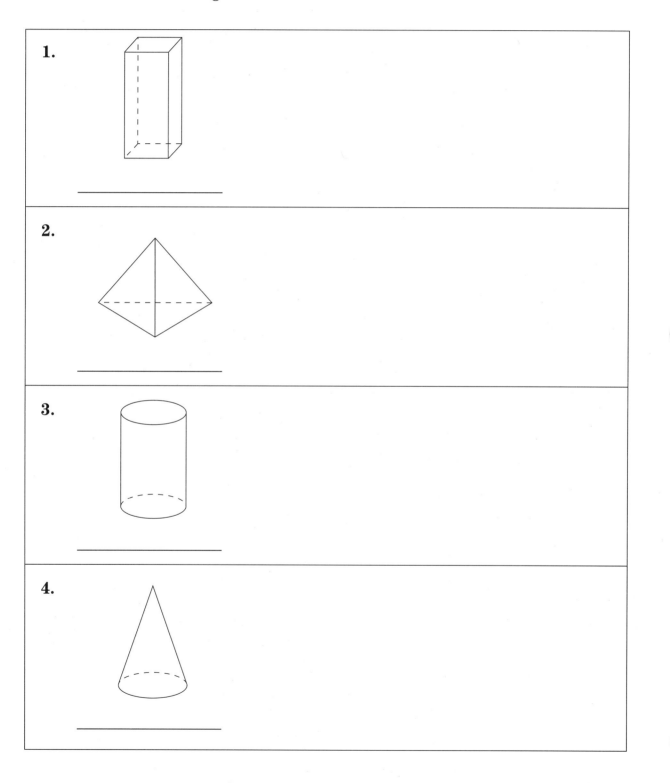

1.

_____

2.

_____

3.

_____

4.

_____

PRACTICE ANSWERS
Page 174

1. C and J
2. A and I
3. E and M
4. F and N
5. B and O
6. D and L
7. G and P
8. H and K

Page 175

9. Square prism
10. Cylinder
11. Square pyramid
12. Cone

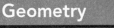

TEST PREP ANSWERS
Page 176

1. Rectangular prism
   Example:

2. Triangular prism
   Example:

3. Cylinder
   Example:

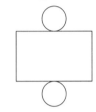

4. Cone
   Example:

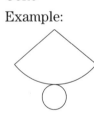

Math at Hand

Wanted In One Piece

OBJECTIVES

- Classify triangles and quadrilaterals according to their properties
- Create "Wanted" posters for specific triangles and quadrilaterals

MATERIALS

- construction paper
- scissors
- crayons or markers

TEACHER NOTES

- In this activity, students are asked to recognize and describe geometric shapes found in the world around them.

- Students should classify and describe the shapes and support their classifications with the appropriate properties for each shape.

- Encourage student creativity for the "Wanted" posters, but mention that the pictures and descriptions of the shapes must be accurate.

- When students make their "Wanted" posters for the rhombus, point out that a square can be considered a special kind of rhombus, having four right angles. Student posters should show and describe a rhombus that cannot be mistaken for a square. This will help them focus on distinguishing characteristics of the shape.

EXTENSIONS

- Have the students measure the interior angles of triangles and quadrilaterals. Investigate the sum of the interior angles for each shape. For quadrilaterals, you may want to begin with the square. The students can easily determine that the sum of its interior angles is 360°. Continue by pointing out that every quadrilateral has interior angles whose sum is 360°.

- Have the students create "Wanted" posters for other figures.

ANSWERS

1. Isosceles triangle

2. Obtuse angle

3. Parallelogram and rectangle

4. Rectangle. Students should mention four right angles and parallel and equal opposite sides to support their answer.

5. The main part of the lighthouse is in the shape of a trapezoid. The door and the light area are rectangles. The window is a square.

6. Isosceles obtuse triangle

7. Parallelogram

8. Check student "Wanted" posters for accurate drawings of the shapes. The description of the right scalene triangle should mention the right angle and the fact that none of its sides are the same length. The description of the rhombus should mention that all four sides are the same length and it has no right angles.

Name _____ Date _____

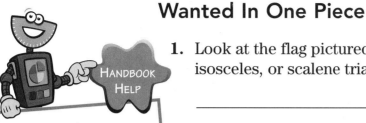

Wanted In One Piece

HANDBOOK HELP

Triangles: 358–363

Quadrilaterals: 364–366

1. Look at the flag pictured. Is the shape an equilateral, isosceles, or scalene triangle? Explain your answer.

_____

2. Look at the triangle at the top of the building pictured. Is the angle at the top of the triangle an obtuse, acute or right angle? Explain your answer.

_____

3. The *Math at Hand* handbook lists five types of quadrilaterals. Which quadrilateral names can be used to describe the shape of the dollar bill?

_____

4. Which is the best quadrilateral name to describe the dollar bill? What facts about the sides and angles of the dollar bill can you use to support your answer?

_____

5. Look at the lighthouse pictured. Name all the quadrilaterals you can find. _____

_____

On the back of this page, sketch each shape based on its description. Identify the type of triangle or quadrilateral.

6. I have three sides, two of which are the same length. My vertex angle is obtuse.

7. My opposite sides are the same length and parallel, but I have no right angles.

8. In the Old West, pictures of outlaws were displayed on "Wanted" posters so that people could help the sheriff catch the outlaw. Using construction paper and crayons or markers, make two "Wanted" posters, one for a right scalene triangle and one for a rhombus. Your poster should include a picture and a detailed geometric description for the shapes so your friends can help you "catch" them.

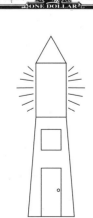

Name _____ Date _____

Problem-Solving Strategies

A restaurant has small tables that seat 4 people. For larger parties, they push the tables together to form longer tables, as shown at the right. How many tables are needed to seat 16 people?

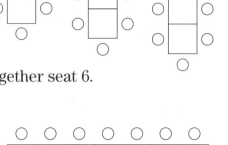

UNDERSTAND

1 One table seats 4 people. Two tables pushed together seat 6.

PLAN

2 You could draw a diagram. Keep adding more tables until there is room for 16 people.

TRY

3 Draw and label the diagram. Count the number of tables needed for 16 people. Seven tables are needed.

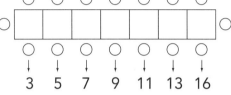

3 5 7 9 11 13 16

LOOK BACK

4 Make sure your diagram is correctly drawn and labeled.

397-403 Solve each problem. Make a model, a diagram, a table, or an organized list, or look for a pattern. Or use guess, check, and revise.

1. An ice cream shop sells double-dip cones that can have two flavors of ice cream. The shop has 2 kinds of cones and 3 flavors of ice cream. How many different double-dip cones can be made? _____

2. In a barnyard there are ten animals—some cows and some chickens. The animals have a total of 26 legs. How many of each animal are in the barnyard?

   _____ cows and _____ chickens

3. Draw the next figure in this pattern. • •• ••• ••••   _____

4. What numbers come next in this pattern? 1, 3, 6, 10, _____ , _____ .

5. Elmo's younger brother built a pyramid with blocks. The bottom layer has 9 blocks. The next layer has 8 blocks, and so on. How many blocks did he use in all? _____ blocks

6. One week a pet store has both dog and cat food on sale. After that, dog food is on sale every third week, and cat food is on sale every fourth week.

   After how many weeks are both pet foods on sale again? _____ weeks

Name _____ Date _____

Suppose your CD case has 4 equal rows. One full row has all your
rock music CDs plus 2 more. One row is short 3 CDs, but the others are full.
You know you have 29 CDs in all. How many rock music CDs do you have?

Since you know the end—how many CDs you have in all—and all the steps,
you can work backward to find the answer.

Now write out the steps in the opposite order, using inverse operations.

Since (29 + 3) ÷ 4 − 2 = 6, you have 6 rock music CDs.

Use any strategy to solve these problems.   **405-408**

7. Lamond bought some bags of potato chips for $1.69 each and
a can of soda for $0.89. He gave the clerk $10. Then he gave
half his change to his brother for washing his bicycle.
He had $2.02 left. How many bags of potato chips did he buy? _____ bags

8. You want to build a fence across the back of your yard.
The yard is 186 feet long. You need fence posts every 6 feet
and they cost $4.50 each. How much will the fence posts cost? _____

Internet access with a local company costs $60
for the hookup and $15 a month after that.
How many months can you keep your Internet
access until you have spent $180?   **407**

9. What is the cost after 1 month?

_____

10. What is the cost after 2 months?

_____

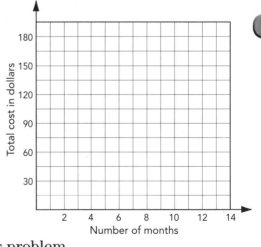

11. Complete the graph at the right to solve this problem.

12. How many months will it take until you have spent $180? _____

Name _____ Date _____

Problem-Solving Strategies

Directions: Use a problem-solving strategy to solve each problem. Show your work.

1. A rectangular kitchen floor measures 12 ft by 10 ft. Lindsey plans to tile the floor with 8-inch square tiles. How many tiles will she need? (Use a diagram to solve the problem.)

3. A baseball player's batting average is .285. In each of the next 10 games, his average goes up .018 per game. What is his batting average after the tenth game? (Make a table to solve the problem.)

2. Morris ordered 4 books from a catalog. Two of the books cost $19.95 each, and 2 of the books cost $8.95 each. The shipping cost for all the books was $7.50. What was the total cost? (Write an equation to solve the problem.)

4. For a play at the theater, tickets for box seats cost $25.00 each and tickets for balcony seats cost $15.00 each. Marvin spent $290.00 for tickets. How many box seats and how many balcony seats did he get? (Use "Guess, Check, and Revise" to solve the problem.)

PRACTICE ANSWERS
Page 180

1. 6

2. 3 cows and 7 chickens

3.
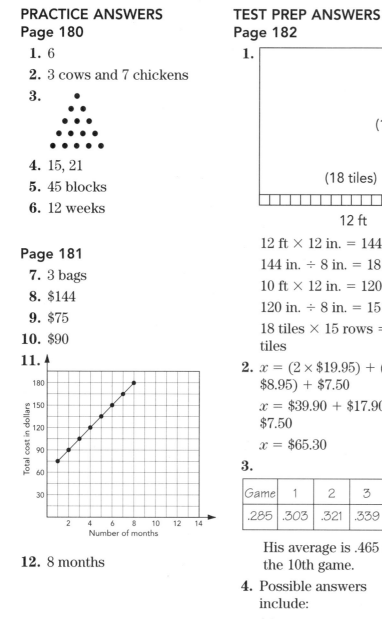

4. 15, 21

5. 45 blocks

6. 12 weeks

Page 181

7. 3 bags

8. $144

9. $75

10. $90

11.

12. 8 months

TEST PREP ANSWERS
Page 182

1.

(15 tiles) 10 ft

(18 tiles)

12 ft

12 ft × 12 in. = 144 in.

144 in. ÷ 8 in. = 18 tiles

10 ft × 12 in. = 120 in.

120 in. ÷ 8 in. = 15 tiles

18 tiles × 15 rows = 270 tiles

2. $x = (2 × \$19.95) + (2 × \$8.95) + \$7.50$

$x = \$39.90 + \$17.90 + \$7.50$

$x = \$65.30$

3.

Game	1	2	3	4	5	6	7	8	9	10
	.285	.303	.321	.339	.357	.375	.393	.411	.429	.447	.465

His average is .465 after the 10th game.

4. Possible answers include:

8 box seat tickets @ $25.00 = $200.00

6 balcony tickets @ $15.00 = $90.00

$200.00 + $90.00 = $290.00

and

11 box seat tickets @ $25.00 = $275.00

1 balcony ticket @ $15.00 = $15.00

$275.00 + $15.00 = $290.00

Name _____ Date _____

Problem-Solving Skills

413-415 These problems are about a party you are hosting. First, circle whether you need an estimate or an exact answer. Next, circle the calculation method you will use. Then solve the problem.

1. You expect to have 158 guests at the party. The caterer is charging $7.95 for each person. What will be the caterer's bill?

Estimate	Mental math	Solution
	Calculator	
Exact	Paper and pencil	

2. You need at least 3 napkins for each guest. Napkins come in packages of 50. About how many packages do you need?

Estimate	Mental math	Solution
	Calculator	
Exact	Paper and pencil	

3. Each table seats 8 people. You want everyone to have a place to sit. How many tables do you need?

Estimate	Mental math	Solution
	Calculator	
Exact	Paper and pencil	

4. You budgeted $60 for flowers. Carnations cost $0.40 each. How many carnations can you put in the centerpiece for each table?

Estimate	Mental math	Solution
	Calculator	
Exact	Paper and pencil	

5. You order two rectangular cakes, each 30 in. by 24 in. What is the largest-size piece you can cut so that everyone gets the same amount of cake?

Estimate	Mental math	Solution
	Calculator	
Exact	Paper and pencil	

6. On the day of the party, you begin decorating at 9:45 A.M. and stay until everything is cleaned up at 10:20 P.M. How much time did you spend?

Estimate	Mental math	Solution
	Calculator	
Exact	Paper and pencil	

413 Circle the most reasonable answer. Explain why you think it is reasonable.

7. You printed 158 invitations on your computer with 6 invitations on each sheet of paper. How many sheets did you use?

26    $26\frac{1}{3}$ 26.33   27

Explain. _____

_____

8. You served 10 gallons of punch at the party. How many 6-oz glasses did you fill?

213    $213\frac{1}{3}$ 213.33   214

Explain. _____

_____

Name _____ Date _____

Find the smallest number that has a remainder of 1 when divided by 2, a remainder of 2 when divided by 3, a remainder of 3 when divided by 4, a remainder of 4 when divided by 5, and a remainder of 5 when divided by 6.

You can try a lot of numbers, or you can use logical reasoning.
- If the number has a remainder of 1 when divided by 2, it must be odd.
- If the number has a remainder of 4 when divided by 5, it must have a 4 or a 9 in the ones place.

Since the number is odd, the number you are looking for must have a 9 in the ones place. So try the numbers 9, 19, 29, and so on, until you find one that has the remainders you need.

$9 \div 3 = 3$ **R0** → NO → $19 \div 3 = 6$ **R1** → NO → $29 \div 3 = 9$ **R2**
                                                                $29 \div 4 = 8$ **R1** → NO →

$39 \div 3 = 13$ **R0** → NO → $49 \div 3 = 16$ **R1** → NO → $59 \div 3 = 19$ **R2**
                                                                 $59 \div 4 = 14$ **R3**
                                                                 $59 \div 6 = 9$ **R5** → YES!

Solve each problem. Use logical reasoning. Look for more than one answer and for unneeded information.

417-418

9. Millford, Newport and Oxiana are all on the same straight road. Millford is 7 miles from Newport and 10 miles from Oxiana. How far is Newport from Oxiana?

_____

10. Yoko has 7 coins in her pocket. They total $0.65. What combination of nickels, dimes, and quarters can she have?

_____

11. How much change will you get from $10 when you buy 2 hamburgers and a large soda?

Hamburgers	$2.99	French fries	$1.29
Hot dogs	$2.29	Small soda	$0.75
Fish Sandwich	$0.99	Large soda	$1.25

_____

12. Jose, Anita, and Rosa are cousins. They have different favorite sports—tennis, golf, and swimming. The two girls don't play tennis, and Rosa has never been to a golf course. What is the favorite sport of each cousin?

_____

_____

13. Of questions 9–12, which ones have more than one answer? _____

14. Of questions 9–12, which ones have unneeded information? _____

Name _____ Date _____

Problem-Solving Skills

Directions: Solve each problem using numbers, words, or pictures. Show your work.

1. Mary Ann is 12 years old. She takes a train trip from Philadelphia to Baltimore. The train leaves Philadelphia at 11:05 A.M. and travels at an average of 40 miles per hour. The train arrives in Baltimore at 12:20 P.M. How long does the trip take?

2. A group of 47 students is going on a field trip. If each car holds 5 students and a driver, how many cars will be needed? (Be sure to check your answer for reasonableness.)

3. Problem: Dennis is 4 ft 9 in. tall. He is 3 in. shorter than Kent. Benny is shorter than both Dennis and Kent. Compared with Benny, how much taller is Dennis?
   What other information do you need to solve this problem?

4. Five students are sitting on a bench. If you are facing the students, Megan is sitting farthest left. Carrie is sitting between Greg and Sue. Chet is sitting next to Megan. In what order are the students sitting? (Note: There may be more than one possible answer.)

5. Coach Barnes has $185.00. She orders 18 T-shirts for the soccer team. Each shirt costs $9.95. Is $185.00 enough for the shirts? (Choose an estimate or an exact amount.)

PRACTICE ANSWERS
Page 185

1. Exact; calculator; $1256.10

2. Estimate; mental math; about 10 packages

3. Exact; mental math; 20 tables

4. Exact; calculator or paper and pencil; 7 carnations per table with 10 left over

5. Exact; paper and pencil; 3 in. by 3 in.

6. Exact; mental math or paper and pencil; 12 hours and 35 minutes

7. 27. 26 sheets is not enough. Fractional parts of sheets of paper make no sense in the context.

8. 213. There was not enough punch to fill 214 6-oz glasses. Since the question asks how many glasses were filled, partially filled glasses are not relevant to the answer.

Page 186

9. Either 3 or 17 miles

10. Either 6 dimes and 1 nickel or 1 quarter, 2 dimes, and 4 nickels

11. $2.77

12. Jose likes to play tennis, Anita likes to golf, and Rosa likes to swim.

13. Numbers 9 and 10 have more than one answer.

14. Number 12 has unneeded information.

TEST PREP ANSWERS
Page 187

1. The trip takes 1 hr, 15 min. (Some information is not needed.)

2. $47 \div 5 = 9\frac{2}{5}$ cars. Since $\frac{2}{5}$ of a car is not reasonable, 10 cars would be needed.

3. You need to know Benny's height.

4. There are 2 possible answers. From left to right:

   Megan – Chet – Greg – Carrie – Sue

   or

   Megan – Chet – Sue – Carrie – Greg

5. Estimate: 20 shirts × $10 = $200, which suggests that $185.00 is not enough.

   Or estimate: $10 × 18 shirts = $180, which suggests that $185.00 is enough.

   18 × $9.95 = $179.10, so $185.00 is enough.

Counting Cones and Cups

OBJECTIVE
• Choose strategies to solve problems involving combinations

MATERIALS
• Math Notebook Page, page 190

TIME
• 45–60 minutes

TEACHER NOTES
• Make sure students know that they are not expected to list each combination when they create the sign at the end of this activity. The sign advertising the store should show that the students understand how to "count" the variety of cones and cups available at the store.

• Encourage the students to be creative when they make the sign for the store. Instead of using the back of the Math Notebook Page, you may want students to use colored paper and markers to make the sign.

• Estimates can be made for the number of combinations before the diagrams, tables, or charts are made. The estimate can then be compared to the actual total.

• Work together with the students to solve a simpler problem using two flavors and two kinds of cones.

EXTENSIONS
• Students can assign costs and a profit margin to the items sold in the store to determine selling prices.

• Students can investigate the choices available in ice cream or sandwich shops nearby and determine the number of combinations available.

ANSWERS
1. Answers will vary. Strategies include Make a Table, Make an Organized List, and Make a Diagram. For this problem, making a tree diagram is a good strategy. Check that the chosen strategy is one that works for the information in the problem.

2. Making an Organized list is probably the best strategy to use. Again, check that the chosen strategy works for the information in the problem and leads to a correct answer.

3. 15

4. Check student responses for good explanations of why particular strategies were chosen.

5. 3 kinds of cones or a cup (4 choices) × 15 ice cream combinations = 60.

6. There are a total of 80 combinations in all. For single-dip servings, there are 5 flavors and 3 kinds of cones or a cup (4 choices). $5 \times 4 = 20$. For double-dip servings, there are 15 possible ice cream combinations and the same 4 choices of cones or a cup. $15 \times 4 = 60$. The signs students create can be creative, and should include the name of the store, "Awesome Edible Icicles." Students can add art or characters to help create a good advertisement for Amy's store.

Name _____ Date _____

Counting Cones and Cups

Amy Arctic is opening a new ice cream store, "Awesome Edible Icicles." Amy plans to offer three different kinds of cones—waffle, sugar, and chocolate-dipped.

1. Choose five flavors of ice cream. Then choose a strategy to show all the combinations of single-dip cones Amy can make. Use the back of this page to display the information. Then write a brief description of the strategy you chose and why you chose it.

Amy thinks that using five flavors of ice cream will result in 25 combinations when they are used to make double dips. You know that since a chocolate/vanilla combination is the same as a vanilla/chocolate combination, there must be fewer than 25 combinations all together. You also know that people will choose to have two dips of one flavor of ice cream.

2. Choose a strategy to show Amy how many different ways there are to combine five flavors of ice cream in double-dips. Show your work on your Math Notebook Page.

3. How many combinations are possible? _____

4. What strategy did you use to display the information for Amy? Why did you choose it?

    _____

    _____

Amy realizes she can sell ice cream in cups as well as in three kinds of cones. Now she wants to know how many combinations she can make for double-dip cones and cups of ice cream using the same five flavors of ice cream.

5. How many combinations are possible? _____

Amy is now ready to make a sign to advertise her new store. She wants the sign to show how many different ways there are to have a single-dip or a double-dip cone or cup of ice cream with five flavors.

6. On the back of your Math Notebook Page, create a sign Amy can use that shows how many combinations will be available at her store.

Name _____ Date _____

My Math Notebook

Topic _____

_____
_____
_____
_____
_____
_____
_____
_____
_____
_____
_____
_____
_____
_____
_____
_____

References to Math at Hand

_____
_____
_____
_____
_____
_____
_____
_____
_____
_____

Examples

_____
_____
_____
_____
_____
_____
_____
_____
_____
_____

References to My Math Book

_____
_____
_____
_____
_____
_____
_____
_____
_____
_____
_____

Name _____ Date _____

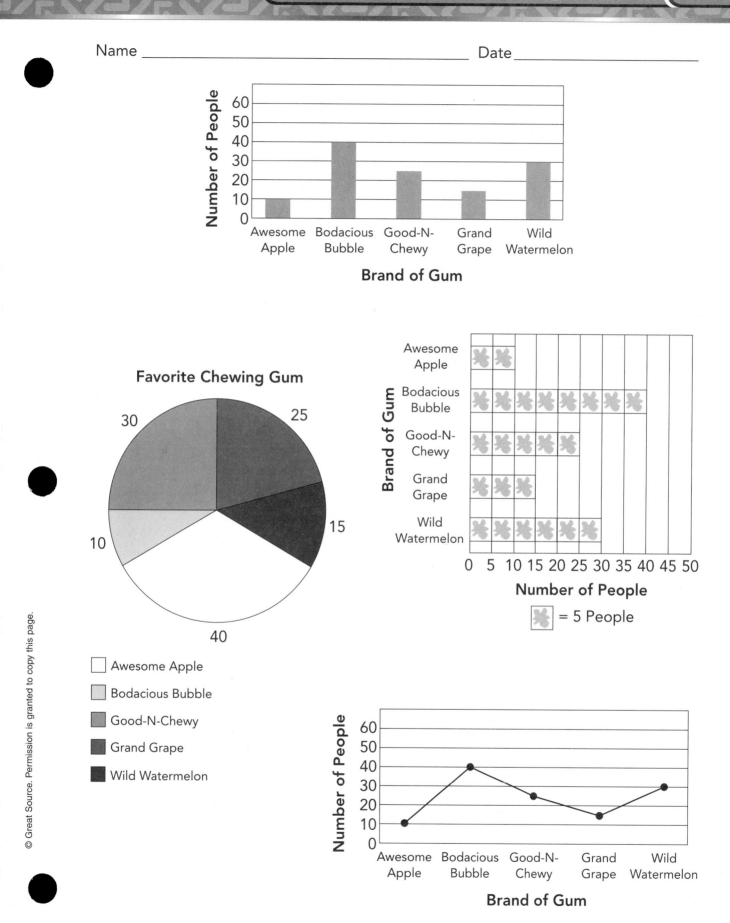

Favorite Chewing Gum

25
30
15
10
40

☐ Awesome Apple
☐ Bodacious Bubble
▨ Good-N-Chewy
▨ Grand Grape
■ Wild Watermelon

= 5 People

Name _____ Date _____

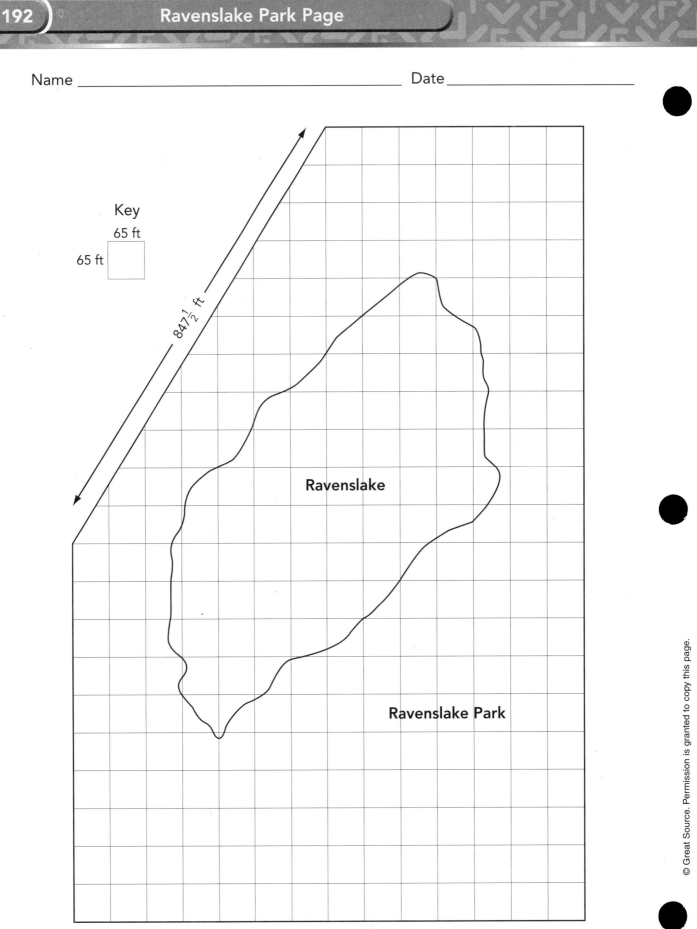

Key

65 ft

65 ft

$847\frac{1}{2}$ ft

Ravenslake

Ravenslake Park